Spring

T0385331

Michael Morpurgo

Spring

The Story of a Season

hodder
press

First published in Great Britain in 2025 by Hodder Press
An imprint of Hodder & Stoughton Limited
An Hachette UK company

The authorised representative in the EEA is Hachette Ireland, 8 Castlecourt
Centre, Dublin 15, D15 XTP3, Ireland (email: info@hbgi.ie)

5

Illustrations by Charlotte Whatmore.

p. 56: 'From Hereabout Hill' by Seán Rafferty. Reproduced
with permission of the Seán Rafferty Estate.
p. 100-101: 'A Song of the Weather'. Words and Music by
Michael Flanders and Donald Swann, Chappell Music Ltd (PRS)
© 1957. All rights administered by WC Music Corp.
p. 145: 'Untitled' by Ted Hughes. Reproduced with
permission of the Ted Hughes Estate.
p. 150: Excerpt from 'Snow Falls', *War Horse*,
written and performed by John Tams.
First performed at the National Theatre, 2007, dir. by
Marianne Elliott and Tom Morris, based on the novel by
Michael Morpurgo, adapted by Nick Stafford.

A CIP catalogue record for this title is available from the British Library

Hardback ISBN 9781399728843
ebook ISBN 9781399728867

Typeset in Sabon MT by Hewer Text UK Ltd, Edinburgh
Printed and bound in Great Britain by Clays Ltd, Elcograf S.p.A.

Hodder & Stoughton policy is to use papers that are natural, renewable
and recyclable products and made from wood grown in sustainable
forests. The logging and manufacturing processes are expected to
conform to the environmental regulations of the country of origin.

Hodder & Stoughton Limited
Carmelite House
50 Victoria Embankment
London EC4Y 0DZ

www.hodderpress.co.uk

For dearest Clare, who shared my spring of 2024, and helped me through to the summer.

Contents

MARCH

The vernal equinox

THERE IS SNOW ON THE HIGH TORS OF DARTMOOR THIS morning. Mountains of clouds are building up over the moor and coming our way. I know it is spring because it is the vernal equinox, and because snowdrops and daffodils and primroses are everywhere. So, it must be officially spring. But it isn't. I know what spring should be and this isn't it.

I live in deepest Devon, between Dartmoor and Exmoor. It is remote and rural, so we can't ignore the weather or the seasons. As tide and wind determine the lives of sailors, so, as country people, farming folk, the seasons determine ours. They determine our lives, to some extent, wherever we live.

I have lived my life mostly in the countryside in England, with occasional forays into town and city. And I am lucky enough to have spent the last fifty or so years living on a farm down a deep lane with high hedges on either side, a lane of potholes and puddles, with grass growing down the middle, a lane that leads only to the River Torridge, which borders the farm, a lane that is fast degrading, becoming a track. As Kipling might have put it, 'Weather and rain have undone it again, / And now you would never know / There once was a road . . .'

Fifty years ago now, I wrote a diary of my first year living down this lane, my first year of working on the land, of farming; I think it was the first year I had really noticed the seasons. It became a book (one of my earliest books). I called it *All Around the Year*. There is a poem by Ted Hughes for each month, with photographs by James Ravilious and drawings by his wife, Robin Ravilious. We were neighbours, all of them better versed than I was in the countryside and in the seasons.

Little has changed. Seasons come and seasons go. They create the pace of our lives, a unifying element for all of us who live here. We see nature and the country-side and farming much as our predecessors did, we live in the same rhythm as they did. We share this place with them, live the same seasons.

We understand what Thomas Hardy meant by 'the old association', that link we forge by living in the footsteps of those who have farmed and lived off the land around us for centuries before us, who made the cottages we live in, who fished the rivers, built and grew the hedges, who planted the trees, who walked where we walk, saw the otters, the herons, the slow worms, the hedgehogs, the rabbits, the foxes and the badgers, who longed for spring as we do, for the sun to warm our backs, for the trees to bud, the grass and corn to grow.

Our work demands that we live much of our lives outside. We like it that way, that's why we are here, why we stay here. It is a difficult place to live in many ways. Everything, except the countryside, is far away – the hospital, the doctor, the shops, the cinema, the swimming pool, the theatre. Satnav often can't find us, and we like that. There are more potholes in our lane than in all the rest of Devon. Only a slight exaggeration.

My wife and I live in a small cottage, built about three hundred years ago. It's a two-up two-down farm worker's cottage. The farm that has been our life, and the lives of our predecessors here, is all around us. They built the cottage of stones gathered from the fields round about, with thick cob walls made of hardened mud and straw – and pigs' blood sometimes, I am told. It has the smallest of windows to keep out the cold, and a thatched roof to keep the place cool in summer and warm in winter.

So, this cottage has become paradise to us, familiar, a place full of memories, of history. Before we lived here, the family pig lived in part of the house, in our kitchen. Years ago, centuries ago, there was a door for the pig and a door for the farm worker and his family.

We knew the old lady, Miss Dovey, who lived here just before us, who had an outside toilet, and lived her evenings in a tent in the living room, because the place leaked so much. We know there was a young lad born in this cottage, who went off down the lane in 1914 to the First World War and never came back. We are conscious that this place has not been paradise for everyone. There was and there is poverty down these deep lanes. We are the lucky generation. The cottage is our hive, our workplace and our home too. We've made it warm and dry, a tea cosy of a place.

Like those who have lived here before us, there are mornings when we hardly have to look out of the window to know how it is outside. When rain thunders down on the roof and lashes at the windows, it's best not to look out. A rhyme from childhood keeps coming to mind. 'Rain, rain, go away, come again another day!' The wind can be constant, from the south-west, not bringing the hoped-for sweet rains of spring, but still fiercer and colder than we'd like.

We idolise spring, of course, because we long for it so much during the dark cold months of winter. Vivaldi was doing the same when he wrote a short poem for each of his *Four Seasons*, as rehearsal notes to inspire his musicians.

March: The vernal equinox

Here, freely translated in my own words, are his notes for Spring, the first movement of *The Four Seasons*. Here's how he remembered it and dreamed of it in his mind's eye.

Spring is sprung. Winter is done.
Sing out, you chirruping birds,
So we know it's true,
Sway and wave, you budding trees.
Show us your glorious green, your early leaves.
Then we will have to believe, that
Spring is sprung and winter is done.

Silver stream in the depths of the wood,
Shine on, run soft.
Hear the distant thunder,
The rumble and crackle and roar.
Feel the cloud shadow, feel the rain.
And now the light of sun again.
Shine on, sweet stream, run soft.

I listen to you, diva blackbird, I see you flitting wren,
I hear you in the trees, drumming woodpecker.
I see you up high, mewing buzzard.
I see you, you hear me.
You sing to me, I sing to you.
We sing in perfect harmony,
For winter is done and spring is come.

Spring

The problem, as we know, is that poor Antonio Vivaldi's joyous Spring in *The Four Seasons* has become so familiar that we only rarely listen to it properly and allow spring to blossom in our minds, as I'm sure he hoped we would. It's become the jolly jingle we hear everywhere, in lifts in hotels, on the phone to the dentist when we're put on hold, in shopping centres to coax us into opening our wallets. His glorious evocation has simply become a cliché, a marketing tool.

For many of us, spring is more often alive with the sound of the jingle-jangle music of a supermarket or shopping centre, that drowns out any birdsong and any wind in the trees, or in a running river. On the back of all this endless noise – so often Vivaldi's 'Spring' – they sell us perfume and toilet paper, air- freshener, shampoo, and dog food. Poor Antonio Vivaldi.

But I digress. Hard to believe sometimes, in the depths of winter, that spring really does happen, that skeletal trees and wind and rain and grey skies do give way to blue skies and rustling green leaves, that it's not a figment of our imagination, not memory and wishful thinking playing tricks on us.

*

The bird feeders are swinging wildly in the wind again this morning, and need filling up. So, I go out to do what has to be done, in my wellies and dressing gown – the birds don't mind. They are loving the Nyjer seeds and the sunflower hearts, especially the goldfinches. And – do not whisper it to the blue tits – the goldfinches are the stars on our bird feeders. They are the smartest-looking birds in the garden, without question. A glimpse of their gold and scarlet and red is sheer joy. And we have more than glimpses. We have a spectacular show outside our window at breakfast every morning. Wondrous.

This is the first year they have come in such numbers, and there are dozens of them – and we have tiny treecreepers, and smart nuthatches, and of course there's always a flurry of blue tits. The great spotted woodpecker, with his flashy red rear, is king of the feeder. When he comes, they all show respect and fly off, temporarily. He's a bit of a show-off, and he's greedy too. It's the goldfinches that enchant.

The robins and the pied wagtails and a pair of faithful collared doves are always there too, to pick up all they can from the leftovers on the ground below – a bonanza for them. They all put on a dazzling aerial show for us outside our breakfast window. It's a flutteringly beautiful ballet we never tire of. The squirrel will try to come sooner or later to interrupt and help himself. He's not welcome. We bang on the window to tell him to get lost. He isn't a bird, he has no right. He's as fat as you like anyway. He's doing OK. And it's a bird feeder!

We long for the end of grey and gloom and the endless dreariness of rain and drizzle, day after day. But we also know that this glorious carnival of birds outside our kitchen window will stop when it does. The birds will come less and less, then, soon enough, not at all. And the absence of birds out there at breakfast will be the first sign for us that the earth is warming, that the intermittent frosts we are still having won't be happening for much longer now, and our birds won't need us so much, and then not at all. They won't come, and we won't feed them, so they won't be there to perform for us. The show will be over till next winter. Spring will have arrived, but we will miss our birds.

After that, we will hear them more than see them. And that's not so bad. The blackbird will lead the chorus from the plum tree in the garden, the crows will cackle and caw as they are buffeted about in the wind. And the robin will want to remind us shrilly who is the king of the garden. But the carnival we have loved and become so used to will be over. The same birds we have been feeding all winter long will be out there, of course, audible sometimes, but mostly invisible. They'll be busy nesting, being

as unobtrusive and secretive as possible, the wrens in their tiny nook in the woodwork above the front door. They come back there each year, to build or rebuild their habitual nest, flitting back and forth with moss in their beaks. We haven't seen them nest-building yet, which is not surprising. They must feel the lingering chill of winter in the wind, as we do. Coats and hats still needed for a while yet.

But at least when spring finally arrives, we won't have to witness again this morning's tragedy, which will haunt us long, I know. We realise that, in part at least, we were the cause of it. I'd only filled the feeders an hour or so before. At breakfast in the kitchen, the feeding show was in full swing out there as we sipped our coffee and downed our hot cross buns. We weren't talking. We often don't talk at breakfast – both of us still too full of sleep and both of us riveted by the frenzied comings and goings around the feeders, by the air-dancing of the goldfinches. Supreme!

The sparrowhawk came from nowhere. We glimpsed it, slicing through the air and plucking a blue tit neatly, clinically, as she tried to lift off the feeder and escape, but too late. He landed with her close by in the long grass under the hedge. We dashed out but there was nothing we could do. The sparrowhawk rose from the grass, the blue tit pinioned in his claws, and was gone.

The violence, the brutal snuffing out of life, the finality of such a death, was not easy to watch, to assimilate, particularly when we knew we had been more than simply witnesses. We had been complicit. Why – if we are being honest – were we still feeding our birds? Was it really to help them through the last days of winter, or was it rather because we simply loved having them there, wanted them to stay, close to us, trusting us, because we so loved the wonder of them?

In the shower afterwards, I continued to blame the tardy arrival of spring. If it had been warmer, if only we'd stopped feeding the birds a week, a day earlier. After all, we knew full well by then that the icy cold of winter was gone and that the birds would not starve, that they could do fine without us. If we had been more aware, then the death we had just witnessed would never have had to happen.

But of course, that wasn't true either. The sparrow-hawk goes on his killing runs whatever the season. All we had done was make it easier for him. And sparrowhawks, like blue tits, have to feed to live, as we do. So, stop angsting, Michael, I keep telling myself. That's life, that's death, that's nature, in tooth and claw. I was still trying to blame the late spring though. A shower is usually a fine place to wash guilt away, to banish or resolve the regrets of life. Writing a confessional piece sometimes helps too.

I've done the shower and I'm doing the writing now, but I'm still brooding on our responsibility. On the other hand, I tell myself, just think of all the cold and hungry birds whose lives we saved by feeding them daily when they needed it all through the winter. Do the sums. One blue tit for twenty goldfinches, and fifty chaffinches, and at least seven woodpeckers, or eight, and all those lovely pied wagtails still trotting about, still dancing, and all those collared doves still cooing.

There now, I feel better. But I'd feel better still to see blue skies chasing the grey and the gloom away. Be gone dull wintry days, be gone miserable rain! It's spring, for goodness' sake!

Less of the Prologue, please.

Hope springs eternal

LAMBING IS, OF COURSE, PLANNED WELL AHEAD. THE rams went in with the ewes months ago, well before Christmas, in the hope that by late February and mid-March spring would have arrived. Mid-March is here.

We can lamb the ewes inside in the barns or out in the fields. Farmers generally prefer to lamb outside if possible, because there is less danger of infection. But if the winter rain and wind linger on, as they have, if there are late frosts, then the risk of lambing outside is far greater. Newborn lambs are all too easily weakened by wet and cold weather. And, inevitably, when first born they are more vulnerable to attack by crows and foxes, and badgers, too. Dogs off the lead can worry and chase them to death. So lambing, whether inside or out, has its risks. Whatever the weather, spring for farmers who keep sheep can be a sleepless and anxious season. Every birth is a potential profit, but also a life.

Even if we lamb indoors, sooner or later ewes and lambs have to go out. And with the ground sodden as it is at the moment, there are going to be tragedies and disappointments. Losing a lamb or a ewe hurts. You have probably known the ewe since birth, a year or two before. You have been there with her as she has her first lamb, helped her through, helped the lamb to breathe, witnessed the first bleating, encouraged the first feeding, lived with the hope that all will be well.

Every spring brings its losses. There have already been a few this year, and that's largely down to this eternal rain. So, it is a struggle we are living through, a struggle between eternal hope and eternal rain. I put on the Beatles CD today to hear my favourite song of hope, 'Here Comes the Sun'. I listen to it often when I'm feeling low. Rain and grey skies and lamb losses, and all the news of war and suffering going on in the world, sometimes combine to dash hope, bring on despondency.

Listening to that song, as I just have, going out in the half-dark of early morning to hear the dawn chorus, and then later watching the birds flying in again, and fluttering on and around the feeder at breakfast, helps drive away the gloom. The sun will come. It must. Today might be the day it happens. The sun might break through, warm us, and warm the ewes and lambs, the early buds and bees. But then I've been hoping for all that for a while. Despondency has a habit of hanging about. I'm wary of it. I put *The Four Seasons* on next. That's better, much better. Music is not just the food of love, it's the food of the spirit.

I've been away, up to the Borders to Scotland for a day or two on a short book tour for World Book Day. Dry and sunshine up there. Sheep bleating happily everywhere. And they really are everywhere you look. The hills of Scotland are alive with sheep, safely grazing, bleating sheep and skipping lambs. Not fair, not fair. Mind you, they've had to endure hard winters up there, much more snow than we ever have in Devon. So, they deserve a spring that's on time.

I went out for a walk after the school event, along a wonderful sandy beach in North Berwick that stretched for miles north and south, wherever I looked. Glorious. And more glorious still, I felt the warmth of the sun on my back for the first time this year. There were crocuses and snowdrops everywhere, carpets of them. If warmth like this has come to Scotland, I thought, it will surely come to Devon. I enjoyed World Book Day in a wonderfully positive school with hundreds of children. Heartwarming it was, to be with so many children in the springtime of their lives, and then in an inspired bookshop in St Boswells. So, I had the bleating of lambs and the joy of books and of children's laughter all in one day. Oh lucky man.

And when I came home the lambs were out in temperamental sunshine, and bleating like their Scottish cousins. There was still a fine Devon drizzle in the air, but it was a warm rain, not cold anymore. I shall go on my river walk again this afternoon along the banks of the Torridge, to see if the bluebells in our wood are showing signs of appearing. It's probably still too early for them, but I can hope. I love to try to spot the first bluebell of the year.

*

The news on the lambing is better today. Lots of twins and even a triplet or two, and one or two lambs skipping about in the sunshine, doing that springing up and down that lambs do off four legs. That's the first time I've seen them doing their capering about this year. I can see that, like me, they are beginning to feel the warmth on their backs. And when they bleat, it is the bleating of contentment. They are running to feed, and suckling hungrily, urgently, tails wiggling and waggling like crazy. And I saw one of them standing up there on his mother's back, surveying the field about him, and the sky all around, and then he was looking back at me. I was leaning there on the gate, and like the lamb taking in the whole new world. It is new every day. I could hear a bee humming somewhere nearby. Now, that really is the music of spring. I hummed 'Here Comes the Sun', for the bee, for the lamb, for me, for fun.

It is at this time of the year that I find I am seeing the farm about me more and more as an interested observer, sometimes a passionate observer, but it's no longer my place of work. I know when I'm out on my regular walks around the farm that memory plays a major part in how I am relating to the natural world about me. My memory tells me an uncomfortable truth, that like it or not I am becoming more distanced these days from the work of the farm, from how I used to spend my days when I wasn't writing full-time. Age can be distancing. Memories can fade, need to be made again.

Clare and I worked daily, hands-on out on the farm, for twenty-five years, so twenty-five springs, twenty-five lambing seasons. But although our work might have had farming at its heart, we had another reason for doing it, and that was children. Both teachers, Clare founded an educational charity about fifty years ago that we called Farms for City Children, to enable urban children to experience life in the countryside and on a farm for a week of their young lives.

We did this because, as children ourselves, both of us had come to know and love the countryside, Clare in the rolling hills of Devon – exactly where we eventually made our home, and set up the charity, Farms for City Children – and me out on the flat fens of Essex. So, we knew how important such an experience was for all children, especially those whose lives were confined to a city environment. We felt it was the right of a child to know there was this other world out there, which was their world too: a world of nature and wonder, a world that fed us, a world we all had to care about and care for. Over 100,000 children later, the charity has three farms, one in Wales, on the coast in Pembrokeshire, one in Gloucestershire near the River Severn, and here at Nethercott House, the pioneer farm in Devonshire where it all began.

As I'm writing this, the children are out on the field, a group of about ten of them, feeding the sheep behind our cottage. I can hear their chatter and their laughter. I can hear Simon's voice too. Simon Ward is one of the two farmers who work with the children. He is from the family that has been working alongside us in partnership with the charity for all these long years.

Down the road, in the fields nearer Nethercott House – where the children and their teachers live for their week with us – two other groups of about ten children each, all from the same school, will be out working. They will be busy helping our other farmer, Adam Bratt, with more lambing. They'll be out feeding the pigs and feeding the cattle in the sheds, while another group, with Katy Martin, the Farm School Manager, opens up the poultry and grooms the horses, and mucks out the stables.

Children play a full and purposeful role out on the farm. They are the reason we came to live here, why this farm and the countryside and all the people round about have been at the heart of our lives for the last fifty years. We have come to know farming and wildlife, and every field and hedge and stream on the farm through the children. In being their guides to this new world for the children for so many years, Clare and I were daily in touch with the seasons and the birds, the wildflowers and trees, with the work on the farm, engaging the children in all we did.

Now in our eighties, we are no longer out on the farm all day and every day with them as we once were. Katy and Adam and Simon and many other wonderful helpers and volunteers do that. But we do go often on our own walks down to the river, along the water meadows and up through the woods. We see the children out at work, planting trees, collecting logs, working in the vegetable garden. They do all sorts, anything the farm needs within the bounds of safety.

So, to know how things are out there these days for the working people on the farm, we have to ask Katy and Adam and Simon – and the children of course. Much of my record of this spring will be coming to me through their eyes, through their daily work on the farm. At the moment, the mud and the wet and the cold, and fatigue, dominate everything they are telling me. They long for proper spring, as we do – rather more than we do, I think, but then they have good reason. They are out in it, not as I am, for recreation or exercise or even for contemplation or dreaming up stories. They are out there because it's their work, and child or adult, they are all farmers together, and they know it has to be done. And anyway, in our long experience, children love being busy, love feeling useful and needed, and they especially love mud and muck. Both are magic for a child!

Adam keeps a record of his days out working with the children and the animals. It's with him they often see a lamb being born for the first time in their lives. It's with him or with Simon that they witness the struggle for life, the joy of a successful lambing, the great sadness when it is not.

Each yesterday, today and tomorrow is a day the children will never forget, a typical farming day that may not seem to be at all springlike, but is nonetheless springtime as it often truly is out in the countryside and on the farm. Their song of spring, as they will remember it, may be a rather different tune from Shakespeare's in *As You Like It*. But it's good to remember that he too walked the countryside. He too had memories he never forgot. Otherwise, he could never have written this:

It was a lover and his lass,
With a hey, and a ho, and a hey nonino,
That o'er the green cornfield did pass,
In springtime, the only pretty ring time,
When birds do sing, hey ding a ding, ding;
Sweet lovers love the spring.

*

A dry frosty start to a day. Checking the ewes in the dark of the early hours, they found a ewe who had chosen to lamb out on the cold concrete, rather than in the barn. Who knows why? She could easily have gone in under cover and lain down in the deep straw bed of the barn, but she chose otherwise, maybe to be alone. The ewe was fine. Her deep fleece was edged in crispy frost, but she was warm to the skin. The lamb, though, was dangerously chilled. They scooped up the lamb, and the ewe followed her back into the barn, the lamb bleating tremulously. A vigorous rub-down was what she needed, and then attentive licking by the mother. Within a minute or two she was up and nosing for the teat.

Evening chores for the children on the farm at this time of year always include feeding the cows. The cattle have been in the shelter of the barn and the yard since November, since when the land has become far too wet for the cattle to go out. If this endless rain goes on, they could be in for another six weeks or so, which is expensive on hay and straw. And the cows much prefer to be out. Animals don't like being cooped up and the farmers, young and older, don't like to be endlessly mucking out.

Of an evening, we know the children are on their way to feed the cows before we see them. Chatter and laughter carries far. The cows hear them coming. They're up on their feet, knowing that the arrival of the children is good news. They are ready and waiting, pushing and shoving one another, heads reaching out through the bars of the feeders. The children carry the slices of hay and drop them down under the cows' noses, making sure there's enough for each one. There's no holding back. The cows are into their hay with a will, happy to have the children's hands ruffling their heads. The children talk to them as they look on, each deciding which is their favourite.

'Mine's got browner eyes than yours.'

'Yours is licking right up into his nose. Disgusting!'

'So? She's got browner eyes than yours. And anyway, yours is a boy, Simon said so. Boys like you do that kind of stuff.'

Spring

We have had some years when the children couldn't be here on the farm – during the year of foot-and-mouth and, more recently, during Covid. It was for us as if the swallows had stayed away, as if the seasons didn't happen. The world was out of kilter. How good it is for us to have the children back here again. And spring on the way, at last, hopefully.

Loveliest of trees, the cherry now

Snowdrops and primroses and daffodils are the great beguilers. They have been nodding away in hedge-rows and on banks and verges everywhere on the farm and beyond for some time already. They herald the spring, they promise it, they try to assure me spring is here. But they do not bring it, not yet. Promises, promises. Only more blue skies, and more days of sunshine and warmth, will do that.

And the trees here in Devon certainly know that too, and are more than usually slow this year, too shy maybe, or too sensible, in this continuing cold to show their buds and their blossom. They're still half asleep, dreaming of warmer days. Up in London, where I was recently, there was blossom blooming everywhere in the gardens and in the parks, magnolia, cherry, camellia, all proclaiming to me, as I passed by, how much earlier and at present more glorious they are than their country cousins. But bitterness apart, they were a wondrous sight, the first fully fledged show of blossoms I've seen this year. My pangs of envy lingered long, envy that city folk can enjoy their spring already, maybe two weeks ahead of us, while we can still only long for it.

Back home, I was straining to find any evidence of buds on the young trees we planted last year, of early blossom on the wild cherry trees in our garden. I think the birds feel the same sense of disappointment. They are still rather too keen to come to our feeders – the two woodpeckers and the nuthatch should be happier feeding in and around the trees by now. I yearn to see that early sheen of young green leaves every afternoon on my walk, as I look out at the forest of oaks on the far side of the river. But the lingering cold will not let the trees bud as they should. They have still the look of winter about them.

I felt full of frustration walking my way back home through 'Bluebell Wood', as we call it. Above me, the beech trees were leafless. And looking about, I knew it would be a while before we see the blue of bluebells. The green shoots were there, trying hard to grow, so the blue will be there, but not soon. When the bluebells do at last come into their own, when the wood is filled once again with their colour and their scent, then I'll know winter is well and truly behind us, that the same spring that inspired Vivaldi's music, and Shakespeare's poetry, is here again.

I chose my usual place at the top of the wood to speak my thoughts out loud. I stopped by the badger sett at the top of the woods, leaned on my stick, and told the trees about what I thought of them, and the badger down in his sett, if he was listening.

'Why are you being so slow to leaf, and so slow to blossom? London's way ahead of you!' One old beech tree above me creaked her response. I got the message. 'We'll leaf when we are good and ready, when we want to leaf, and we'll blossom when we want to blossom. Got it? Stop hassling us.'

I talk in the woods quite often, quietly, and often not directly to the trees or to invisible badgers, but to myself. Sometimes, I even tell them the stories I'm dreaming up. It's strange, but the more I touch them and talk, the more time I spend in among them, the closer I feel I come to know and understand them, the stronger my connection, the stronger my affection. I do hug trees, I do lean on their companionship. I know them, and they know me. I'm in those woods more than anyone. They're used to having me around. So I can joke and tease, and feel they don't mind.

I often sit down and lean back against their trunks to listen to them. I have even done what bears, I know, do sometimes in the forests of Canada and other wild places.

I rub my back up against them to satisfy an itch. I've become ever more fascinated by wrinkles in their bark. The deeper the wrinkles the older they are, of course, like elephants, like me. And in among the trees in Bluebell Wood I can talk, or even shout; I can cry, too. It's a holy place to me, precious, private. As woods have often been to people over the centuries. Like a church, but better in a way. No priest, no judging. I listen to the whisper of the trees, and they listen to me. I must have touched every tree in Bluebell Wood by now, over the last fifty or so years. They are good companions to me, they shade me against the heat, shelter me from storm and wind from 'the slings and arrows' of life.

It's a place of memories. I must have walked there with all of my family over the years, young and old, spring, summer, autumn, winter, the children then the grand-children and now the great grandchildren, running on ahead, skipping and leaping, their whooping filling the woods. I've led thousands of our city children through the trees on our Sunday walk. It's a play-forest to them, a place of fairy tales, where Little Red Riding Hood lives, where the Wolf lives, where the three bears live, where Hansel and Gretel come, where witches live. It's a stage set for all kinds of stories, so a place of wonder and fear and beauty, a place to hurry through when the wind soughs and shakes the branches, a place to stop and gaze at the bluebells when they are there, a place to catch a glimpse of a fox darting away, or a couple of startled deer drinking in the stream then springing away; or maybe simply to pause and stay silent, all of us, by the badger sett, waiting and longing for him to emerge – he never does, of course. But they know he's listening down there, and so do I.

But these days I walk there alone mostly, alone with my memories, and thoughts and dreams and stories. One tree I make a point of passing by sometimes is very special. I visit it often. I worked with our dear friend David Ward, Simon's father, for most of my adult life. He and his family taught us our farming. He was the farmer who owned the fields and barns all around, and Bluebell Wood too, looked after the trees and loved them. He carved his initials, with his future wife's, into the trunk of a young beech tree on the day he and Daphne became engaged, many decades ago. Now it is the most magnificent beech tree in Bluebell Wood.

David died suddenly, too young, a great loss to us all. Best of friends he was, and a true countryman. He loved his family and his farm and his animals, and Bluebell Wood especially. David was for more than forty years the heart and soul of the farm, and of Farms for City Children. For the thousands of children who stayed with us he will always be 'Dave the farmer', with a ready smile and a cheery quip. Children thought the world of him. I hear his laughter in the woods more than anywhere else.

Spring

I don't think I ever walk through Bluebell Wood without thinking of him.

Shakespeare was right. He usually is. Looking up into the leafless branches of the beech trees, they are indeed still 'bare ruined choirs where late the sweet birds sang'. But I know, and they know in their own way too, that the sap is rising, their winter days of hibernation are coming to an end again, the lifeblood is coursing through them. They creak with age, as I do. They lean in the wind as I do. They shiver with cold as I do. And today as I came out of the woods into the fields and saw the lambs cavorting – they really do skip – I felt the trees believe, as I do, that spring is springing. I can smell it in the air. I've seen the early swelling of the buds in some low-slung twigs when I looked more closely. I may have to imagine it for the moment, but the vibrant green of their new leaves is bursting to break out, and when it does, Bluebell Wood will shake itself out, find again a new life, and every tree I've just walked by will sing and sway and dance again to the music of spring. It won't be long now.

*

As I come home over the hill, with Dartmoor in the distance cloaked in cloud, I can hear the sound of children's voices down in the valley below, the valley of the Okement river. The farm is bordered by two rivers, the Okement and the Torridge. The Torridge is the river where Tarka the Otter lived, the water meadows where the writers Henry Williamson and Ted Hughes and Seamus Heaney walked, where I set my story of *War Horse*, where, in my mind's eye, Joey spent his working life as a farm horse before he went off to the First World War.

I find my way over the fields towards the sound of the children, thinking of Ted Hughes, who loved fishing for salmon and sea trout in the Torridge, and who used to come to read to the children sometimes of an evening. I think of how he loved trees and all that was wild and free in the countryside. He'd have been so pleased to discover what the children are still up to after so long. Today, they are all out with Adam planting trees. Later in my walk, I stood at a distance and watched them, all of them digging, planting carefully, heeling in gently afterwards, putting up the guards to help the saplings survive the nibbling of deer and rabbits. It's a perfect time for planting, the ground full of the moisture the young trees will need. The sooner the better, they will need the warmth to help the roots to spread and grow to give them a good start.

It was a joy to watch the children who, like the saplings they were planting, also need nurturing and encouragement to grow well. They need a good start, and part of that should be an early connection to the natural world about them, so they can feel a sense of belonging to it and responsibility for it, for the tree they are planting. Every one of those trees, I was thinking, will only be there helping the earth to breathe and heal, and grow, because one of those children from a school in Walsall planted it. In twenty years maybe, when they have themselves grown well and tall, they can come back and see their tree, as so many children have already done over the years. Those trees will blossom as they will.

So, I'm feeling full of the joys as I wend my way home through the fields still heavy with mud, in wellies heavy with mud too, along the lane where the potholes are still puddling the lane. The joy in my heart makes light work of the mud and the puddles as I trudge homewards.

And then . . . then, as I come in through our gate, with the rain coming on again, I stop to look at the little oak tree we planted the year before last, that we hope will one day be a great oak like its great great great great etc etc great grandparent, called King Offa's Oak, from Windsor Great Park, a descendant of one of the very oldest oaks in England. I was looking for an early bud on twigs that will one day be great branches. And I found two! Two!

Fragile, tentative twigs maybe, and the buds little more than minute suggestions. But buds they are, budding buds, beautiful buds.

Then, as if that wasn't joy enough for one day, and with my wellies now light with laughter, I walked into the garden and there was the cherry tree we planted at about the same time as the oak. And on the tree it looked as if there might be blossom, just a wisp of it. I went closer. Blossom! Definitely blossom! Not the voluminous, voluptuous, vulgar, volcanic explosions of blossom that I'd seen a while before in London. Nothing showy about it. This was our little cherry tree, our *Prunus avium* 'Plena' tree, taking its first little steps, and telling us subtly, modestly: 'Look at me! I'm here again, putting on my blossom, doing my best to strut my stuff, to put on the style. It may not be much just yet, but you wait and see. Don't you give up on me! I may be little, I may be late, but I'm here, please look at me.'

Clare and I had a cup of tea looking out from our kitchen at our cherry tree that is trying so hard to blossom, and we remembered a poem in *Where My Wellies Take Me*, a book we'd put together a few years ago. It's a poem we love, so sitting there we read it again, out loud, but not loud, softly. Seemed a good moment, appropriate.

Spring

Loveliest of trees, the cherry now
By A.E. Housman

Loveliest of trees, the cherry now
Is hung with bloom along the bough.
And stands about the woodland ride
Wearing white for Eastertide.

Now, of my threescore years and ten,
Twenty will not come again,
And take from seventy springs a score,
It only leaves me fifty more.

And since to look at things in bloom
Fifty springs are little room,
About the woodlands I will go
To see the cherry hung with snow.

A walk on the wild side

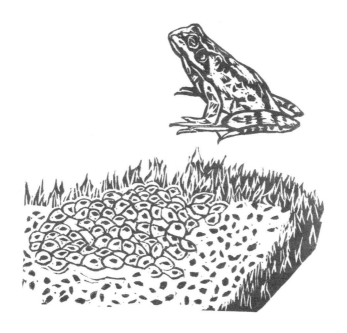

It was the wild garlic that reassured me yesterday on my way back up the farm track from the Torridge, a path that seems steeper to me every year. It was hard going, the walk, and twice the effort when you're walking so much through gluey mud, sliding and slithering on the hills, everything slippy and treacherous underfoot in the woods. I tripped and fell there during the winter, fell heavily on my shoulder and reignited the pain of an old sporting injury from my youth. Old injuries have a habit of returning to haunt you, always unexpectedly.

I knew very well the dead branch that had been my downfall, an old familiar hazard. I slipped on the mud as I was stepping over it. The shoulder still reminds me of that mossy old bough every time I turn over in bed at night. I tread more carefully now, especially over the offending fallen branch, covered ever more, I've noticed, in moss and ferns, disguised deliberately to trip me again if I'm not wary. It's a reminder that every time I go into the woods I must speak or sing softly, so as not to intrude too much into their silence, that it's their place – and I must be careful where I tread too.

Yeats wrote once: 'Tread softly because you tread on my dreams.' I remember that line often as I walk in Bluebell Wood. They are living beings, trees. And we must treat them as such.

The wild garlic isn't flowering yet, but the green of it I'd been seeing everywhere on my walk, under the trees, in the hedgerows, along the riverbank. I was happy enough coming up the path to stop and catch my breath, to pick a leaf of wild garlic as I did, and rub it hard between my fingers, sniff it, smell it, savour it. And there it was, another sure sign that the corner is really turning.

There was other evidence of it on my last walk on the wild side. I'd noticed a small but perfect daisy, her golden eye open to the day, my first daisy of the year, almost lost in the grass of the water meadows. And in the woods I'd seen, in among the promising green of the bluebells-to-be, my first yellow celandine with its shiny petals and heart-shaped leaves, and my first deep-purple violet too. I think I saw a dandelion as well, but it was half hidden deep in a muddy hoofprint, of a cow or a deer – I can't be sure.

Walking is good for wondering. I was wondering as I walked, seeing dandelions and daisies all around, about names, about linguistic origins, how they come about; about the names of flowers, for instance, how you couldn't make them up, but how someone once did, someone must have done. Someone French must have made up dandelion, 'dent-de-lion', lion's tooth. Norman influence, surely. And then there's daisy, that opens at first light and closes at dusk, from 'day's eye', of course. The source might have been some Saxon wag, or an inventive child in the fifteenth century.

And all the fields on the farm have ancient names, Longlands, Heathy Hill, Innocents' Copse, Candlelight Meadow, Cross Park, Rushy Park, Redlands, the original meanings and associations often lost in time. Some links are known. Iddesleigh, the village itself, was Saxon in origin, its name in Old English *Eadwig Leah*. Eadwig may have been the landowner who might have laid the hedges, who cleared and made the fields. Leah means a clearing in Old English. In the Doomsday Book of 1086, the village was called Edeslege.

The place and the names remind me often, mostly on my walks, that for thousands of years people have walked where I walk – the Saxon farmers who first created the hedgerows to enclose their animals, hedgerows that still serve that purpose, that are home and refuge to all the many birds and animals and insects we see today, how they too must have endured the mud and the cold and wind of winter; and have felt and witnessed like I do, on my walks on the wild side, the early hopeful beginnings of spring, that prologue and promise of the summer to come, the promise of warmth, of harvest, of food, of survival.

*

Mid-morning, when I'm writing on my bed, I am called to go downstairs for coffee. Always welcome. And I'm so glad I went down just now when I did. The sun was out. No, honestly, the sun was out! The garden was glowing with busy life. The bumblebees were all over the flower pots outside the kitchen window. They were visiting the hyacinths, purple and white, they didn't care which. It was the first time the bees have been out in numbers. And bumblebees don't lie, and they don't waste their time.

And joy of joys – when I was wheelbarrowing compost onto the vegetable patch, I heard the sound of a buzzard mewing high over Bluebell Wood, looked up and saw two of them circling the thermals, mewing to one another, floating on the air high up in the blue. I haven't heard that for six months at least. They only do that when they're happy, and they're only truly happy when it's warm. Much like us, really.

And it wasn't just the bees telling us we are over the cusp now, that the year really is turning. No more looking back, Michael. That's what spring does. It helps us to look forward, to put the gloom of winter out of our mind. Our wren in the garden is showing us the way. We have a wren, or two, that flits back and forth in under our eaves under the thatch. They can be mistaken for a leftover autumn leaf, blown about in a gust of wind. They are impossibly small, hugely energetic and deeply engaging. When they pipe at you, as they do, I know it is a greeting rather than a warning.

We have watched a family of wrens nesting there for ten years or more, mostly successfully. One year, their nest was discovered and attacked by crows. I really do not like crows. They attack our windows sometimes when they see reflections of themselves, and leave unpleasant messages all over the path to our front door. 'Crow graffiti', I call it. And much worse, they prey mercilessly on the nests of our garden birds, the wrens and wagtails especially.

So coffee time was a good break, full of ideas and full of wonderful surprises. But then I posed a question to Clare to which I should have known the answer. 'Remind me,' I asked, looking out at our wonderful ash tree that dominates the garden. 'Which comes into leaf first? Ash or oak?'

And she replies with one of her wise granny sayings – she has one or two for every occasion, every question. 'Oak before ash, we're in for a splash. Ash before oak. We're in for a soak.' So either way it's not good news then.

Not at all what I needed to hear. 'Never trust a rhyme,' I said. But I knew that there was truth in what she was saying. Most of her granny sayings are full of annoying truths. She's not wrong. It rains in Devon, a lot. And this year, biblically. On this first beautiful day in months, I really don't want to have to think of rain or wind or cold.

After watching our wrens hopefully choosing again their nesting site just outside our front door, after seeing the bumblebees out there hovering over the flowers in blessed warmth at last, all I wanted was to dwell for a while on thoughts of lighter brighter longer days ahead.

So, I came upstairs and read a favourite poem by a dear poet friend of ours, Seán Rafferty, who used to live just down the road from us, and who died thirty years ago now. We miss him still, but we have his words. Clare had known him since she was seven years old. He was like a grandfather to her. He wrote this poem to celebrate the

Spring

coming of spring in this place that we all call home, fifty
or more years ago. We live on the hill he calls Hereabout
Hill.

From Hereabout Hill

From Hereabout Hill
the sun early rising
looks over his fields
where a river runs by;
at the green of the wheat
and the green of the barley
and Candlelight Meadow
the pride of his eye.

The clock on the wall
strikes eight in the kitchen
the clock in the parlour
says twenty to nine;
the thrush has a song
and the blackbird another
the weather reporter
says cloudless and fine.

It's green by the hedge
and white by the pear tree

in Hereabout village
the date is today;
It's seven by the sun
and the time is the springtime
the first of the month and
the month must be May.

May not yet maybe, but May beckons. We remember Seán Rafferty at this time of year especially. He would spend his winters writing his poetry in front of the fire in his cottage just down the lane from Nethercott House, where the visiting children stay. At this time of year, he'd be found up in the walled garden, where he was the vegetable gardener for nearly twenty years. He'd be in his shed pricking out the onions, the sweetcorn, the courgettes. The children would be wheelbarrowing the compost he needed down to the garden and forking it out, digging it in. Seán and the children were always part of the growing in that garden. Sadly, Seán is no longer there, but the children are, and the growing goes on much as it always has done in Seán's garden – as we still think of it.

It's been difficult this year to get on with the growing. I've never known the ground so sodden. But the compost has been wheeled on, and as soon as it's dry enough – just a few successive days without rain would do that – and then we can get in there and dig it in. In the vegetable garden so much is preparation, preparation for spring and planting out. We've been pricking out for weeks now, and the young plants are already growing in the greenhouse. The onions are doing well, the rest a bit slow.

Out in our garden at home volunteers and the children do much of the work, the rhubarb is looking promising, just little pink shoots with crumpled-up leaves at the moment. But the wet does not seem to have bothered it. The blackcurrant plants are doing well already too, growing strongly. And last year's kale is looking tired, but there's enough for us to be going on with for me to make our breakfast smoothie, until the new plants from the greenhouse can go in.

Kale-picking is my first task of every day. I'm out there in my wellies and pyjamas every morning around eight o'clock. The children from Nethercott often go past in the trailer on their way to their first job of the day, checking the ewes and lambs with Simon. If I'm awake enough I give them a wave, and get a dozen back.

In these last days I've loved my early kale-picking sorties into our garden, because of the blackbird. For years there has been a blackbird nesting somewhere in the garden or nearby. I have no idea where. But for years I've been used to having the company of a blackbird in early spring, and I'm supposing, hoping, he's from the same family. He sees me from the holly tree by the gate. And I see him. But we do more than just look at one another.

It's one of the great joys of this time of the year for me that he sings to me. He doesn't sing in winter. But all through spring and summer he's there. He sings out from his branch, and I echo back the same tune as best I can. When he changes his tune, I do the same. He does not caw or cackle, he does not chirp or chirrup, he sings, he performs. He has a huge repertoire of arias he likes to sing to me, and I really feel he likes it when I sing back to him, imitating his melody. It's my way of applauding, of thanking him for being there, and he knows it.

He was up there this morning, singing. So I was singing back, whistling really, when the tractor and trailer and the children went by, waving and laughing at me in my wellies. Once they'd gone, my blackbird simply went on singing louder than ever. I think he thought the waving must have been for him. He had the wonderful voice, but I was the one in wellies. So we share the applause. It was a moment. And Clare said at breakfast that my smoothie – of kale, banana, apple, pear, flax and chia seeds, ginger and sour cherry juice – was supreme. I thought so too. More applause. I like applause.

*

Spring

This morning has confirmed to me that we are in a new season. I put on my *Four Seasons* CD again and played Spring to celebrate. Vivaldi has the mood so right. Wherever I go now, out in the garden, on my walk, whenever I look out of my window, I know winter is over and done. The lambs in the fields all around are growing fast, the early ones almost small sheep by now. The buzzard mewing up there is back again this morning. I see more rabbits scuttling away into the hedgerows. The wrens are here or hereabouts all day, reconnoitring their future home near our front door, so we now use the kitchen door instead so as not to disturb them.

Yesterday, there was the occasional daisy or dandelion or celandine. This afternoon there were hundreds, thousands. Duck flew off the river in noisy numbers, not alarmed at my approach, just letting me know this was their river, their sky, that I should watch how they fly, how they circle, and come back to reclaim their river further down.

A heron lifts off prehistorically from the far shore, where the river swirls and turns and runs fast and urgent over the rapids, as if not wanting to be confined anymore between the banks, as if not to be overshadowed by the alders and willows, longing only to reach the wide sea all those miles away at Bideford.

Ever changing, ever moving, the river is our lifeblood, taking away the rain that falls on our land, that grows all we need, all nature needs, then flows it out to sea to return in time as rain again to refresh and revive. We take our rivers for granted at our peril. Only stop and stare and wonder and think, and we know it. I've been grumbling on about how much rain we've been having, how hard it is to trudge through mud. Stop your grumbling, Michael.

Mud is fine, mud is cool. I love mud. Hippos love mud. Elephants love mud. What is there not to love? What is mud but earth and water, earth that is useless without water. On my happy walk home through the lovely mud, through all that 'mud, mud, glorious mud' – I hum the tune as I go along – I come to the deepest puddle on the whole farm, a pond more than a puddle. It ponds out from the gateway into the fields where Wood Hill comes down to meet the water meadows. If I wade through too fast it will lap over the top of my wellies and I'll get wet feet. I go slow. I hate walking with wet feet.

As I struggle to open the gate I happen to glance down and see it. Frogspawn! Clumps of it, floating like grey slimy sponges on the surface of the puddle. I crouch down to be close to it, to witness the beginning of new life, many new lives. I know there are multiple dangers ahead for them, the heron, the puddle drying up too soon, a cold snap of late frost. I shall be careful where I tread down there in the days ahead. I wish them well, and wend my way up the hill, through Bluebell Wood and homewards, taking my time to stand and stare and wonder, reflecting that frogs need water too. We all need water.

MAY SOON

'In my mind's eye'

On a fine day like today, it is still light enough to think of it as daytime at 6 p.m. And it's not just me who is noticing this. The whole world about me is becoming brighter with colour, chirpier with every day that passes. To try to flourish, remain positive throughout the short winter days, with the long dark evenings, with the world outside grey and harsh, cold and inhospitable, is often hard, and if prolonged – which it most certainly has been this year – can be deeply inhibiting to our sense of well-being. We need the daylight and warmth of spring to renew our optimism, to cast away the shadows. And so does the natural world about us. Every creature and plant and tree out there is gradually growing, beginning to fulfil itself, and is rediscovering its purpose in being, to play its part in this new beginning.

The winter has been, to some extent, as much of an enforced hibernation for them, as much of a struggle for them, as for us. People, old people especially, still die more in winter, of cold or hunger, as we historically always have. Spring, summer, autumn, winter, we're all in this together, and we should never forget it.

Seasons are the tides of our lives. We have to adapt to the rhythm of each day. For so many of us, it's not easy, not natural anymore, we are predominently urban these days. We have become distanced from the seasons, as we have from nature herself. For so many reasons, for our well-being, for the planet, we need to revive that connection.

We are certainly more aware now of our vulnerability to climate change, of the vagaries of extreme weather. This affects the natural world every bit as much. We are all endangered together. The seasons are the great reminders of our reliance on the rhythm of life on this planet, the rhythm of our own lives; Shakespeare's Seven Ages, that encompass birth, life and regeneration and death, remind us uncomfortably of the truth of this, from infant mewling and puking to the end of life, sans teeth, sans eyes, sans taste, sans everything.

So we know that everything does have its season, and we are now in the season of new life, of regeneration, of hope. It is a time of transition. I see all around me, especially in Bluebell Wood, the evidence of last autumn and the winter we are leaving behind us, the fallen branches everywhere after the storms of winter, the carpet of beech mast I crunch through every day, and everywhere the brown and yellow of dead autumn leaves lying scattered in among them, or in wind-blown piles up against the hedges.

But today, as every day now, and everywhere in the woods, I notice the proliferation of early green leaves of bluebells coming through, slowly but surely overwhelming this last litter of winter and autumn, covering and hiding it. Green for now, blue entirely soon enough, they're taking over the forest floor and making it their own. There is new growth everywhere I look, of catkins and pussy-willow, wild anemones – or windflowers – violets and speedwell, primroses, more primroses, and even one early purple orchid.

*

In hedgerows all around the fields I walk through as I make my way down towards the river, the blackthorn heralds the changing of the seasons with a show of sudden white blossom. And the sharp-thorned gorse, that makes the most effective of all hedges, is already turning bright with gold. Stitchwort is there too, climbing in the hedgerows, each flower tiny, white and delicate, as delicate as a stitch. How welcome a sight are these trusty harbingers of spring. The bumblebees are about down here too, in and around the hedges already, on the hunt for nectar.

And it won't be long before the bees discover the apple orchard our neighbours have planted recently, further up the Torridge towards the confluence with the Okement. I walk often through this infant orchard, and can see how well it's coming on. The young trees are doing fine. A few have been damaged by deer, who of course love to nibble on freshly planted saplings. But they have been well protected, and most have survived their first two springs. One or two of them have been knocked over or washed away by the river in flood, and there has been a lot of flooding this year. The river has been bank-high for most of the winter, so flooding has been frequent and powerful, taking some of the newly planted apple trees with it. But not too many, considering.

It's a good thought as I walk through, that there'll be hundreds of new fully grown apple trees down here in a year or two, and indeed for decades after that, and that it won't be long before they'll be out picking apples every autumn. And it won't be long either before we'll be seeing a field of apple blossom every spring. There are a few of them showing the beginnings of blossom already. It's not hard to imagine a time when families will be out there picking the apples, among them maybe grandpas like me telling grandchildren proudly and repeatedly how it was them who planted the trees.

I've written a poem about an apple tree and a grandfather. It helps that I am one. It's in honour of our neighbours, the Longthorne family, who so kindly helped us through the pandemic time, who made a pathway through their apple trees for me to walk along the river. It's in honour too of their trees, and in honour of all grandparents, who can sometimes – so I'm told – repeat themselves, and in praise of the patience of grandchildren who have to put up with us.

Whacks of apples

'I planted that tree.
See this photo of me?
In the garden, I am,
Aged five or six, I suppose.
Who knows? Me in my wellies,
Seaside spade in hand,
But it wasn't sand I dug.
It was earth.
I dug that earth. I planted that tree.'

'You told me, Grandpa. You told me.'

Spring

'An apple tree, he was,
Bramley apples. Bestest apples.
Makes the bestest crumbles and pies,
No taste like them,
Not in the whole wide world.
That tree, he didn't grow apples for a year or two –
You have to wait for the good things in life.
Waited long enough for you, I did.
I dug that earth. I planted that tree.'

'You told me, Grandpa. You told me.'

'Buds of hope bloom into blossoms,
The busy bees are flying in,
Full of the joys of spring, they are.
But nippy and deadly comes a late white frost.
Then blossom don't blossom,
No bees will fly, no apples will grow.
Sad for my tree and the apples, sad for me.
Always another year, I say.
I dug that earth. I planted that tree.'

'You told me, Grandpa. You told me.'

'He leans these days, my dear old tree.
Much like me, much like me.

May soon: 'In my mind's eye'

But look at him now, still standing there.
Not straight, but strong, through wind and storm.
Home to all his birds and bugs,
Home to you and home to me.
What songs he sings! How he rustles and roars!
I dug that earth. I planted that tree.'

'You told me, Grandpa. You told me.'

'And look at the apples he's grown us this year.
Whacks of them, like they used to say.
Never seen them so big, nor so green, nor so red.
How heavy they hang, how his branches droop.
He has tired himself out, had quite enough.
He's done his job, now we must do ours.
You climb up and shake them all down
But gently mind, gently. I'll catch what I can.
I dug that earth. I planted that tree.'

'You told me, Grandpa. You told me.'

*

The ground was definitely firmer everywhere under my
feet as I went on my walk today. No rain now for three

days makes a huge difference. In the lane, I even spotted two sparrows enjoying a dust bath! They love a bath when it's in water, splashing about as they do, but in a dust bath they frolic. It's an ecstatic dust dance. The mud must definitely be retreating. The frogspawn is still there in the puddle by the gate at the bottom of Wood Hill, but it's a smaller puddle now, not almost a pond as it was. I worry that the heron I see frequently down on the river, just across the water meadows, might pay the puddle a visit. They have eyes as sharp as any hawk, and they're known to be very partial to frogspawn, and frogs.

It was a few springs ago when I last found frogspawn in the same place. I feared then that the puddle might dry out before they could hatch, so I decided to scoop up the frogspawn and carry it in a bucket back to our pond in the garden at home, but it was not a successful rescue. Word must have got around the heronry to come looking in our pond, or maybe the newts that live there did the damage – they like frogspawn and tadpoles – but we had no more frogs around the garden that year than usual. So this spring, I'm leaving the frogspawn where it is and hoping, hoping that the puddle does not dry out too quickly, before the tadpoles can hatch out, before the heron discovers the frogspawn. Nature will have its way – I've learned that from feeding the birds in the garden. Best not to interfere.

I can see that the full glory of spring won't be long now. The oaks and willows and alders at the water's edge on both sides of the river will soon be clothed in the new green of spring. I really thought I saw an early sheen of green today. One day soon, I tell myself, and the early leaves will be there. I long now to see the end of all skeletal trees, winter trees.

A memorable walk I had by the river today. I saw a kingfisher flash by, waited a while for the chance of another sighting. I see a kingfisher only very rarely. But when I do it's a wonderful moment to savour, a privilege to witness. It was a brief moment, but a glimpse is enough, all you need. The kingfisher is the jewel of the river. And walking a little further on, close to the river's edge, high on the muddy bank, I looked down by my welly and spotted an otter spraint. I crouched down. It was black, shining, and fish-smelling on my fingertip. So I had two very different but momentous moments of connection today with perhaps the two most iconic creatures of the river, kingfisher and otter.

The presence of both kingfisher and otter gives me some hope for the river. We need more than hope, of course. When we first came to live here fifty years ago, we could and did swim often in the Torridge river. The city children from Nethercott used to love it. You wouldn't do it now. It is simply too polluted. We have, all of us, used and abused our rivers in this country over many decades, farmed around them too intensively, poured our sewage into them, extracted water from them, overfished them, neglected them.

Our wildlife needs clean water. We need clean water. Fish need clean water too. There just aren't the numbers of cormorants or egrets or kingfishers or herons on our river or any river as there used to be, because there isn't the number of fish that there used to be. This can and must be put right, for their sakes, for all our sakes.

Many good and right-thinking people, locally and nationally and globally, are trying to repair the damage. So we mustn't despair. Being downhearted about it doesn't help. This new generation of young people is much more aware. We are all much more aware. I am more aware. We may have been slow to understand the damage we have done. We understand now. We have to undo the damage we have done, for the kingfisher, for the otter, for the fish, for the heron, for the frogs, for the bees, for us all, and for our children.

Otters and kingfishers and herons, all of them, are still here. They haven't given up on us, as they had every right to do. So we mustn't give up on them. Only a short time ago, for the first time of walking the river in fifty years, I did see an otter, and not just the spraint of one as I saw today, which was exciting enough. I saw my very own

Tarka. I sometimes think he came to see me. I see him again every day 'in my mind's eye', as the Bard once put it. It's a memory I will carry with me all my life, so long as I have a memory.

The river was not in full spate, but flowing fast, the current in the middle racing along. In under the bank was the only calm water. I was on my way home, about to turn away from the river and up the track, when I saw it out of the corner of my eye. I thought at first it must be the tail of a salmon I was seeing, a salmon diving, just disappearing, which was exhilarating enough. I stood there as still as a heron, watching to see if it would come up again.

It didn't, but an otter did. Right below me under the bank, in the still water, there he was, chewing away contentedly, and looking up at me as he was feeding, seemingly quite unconcerned that I was there. I could hear the crunch of him eating – it looked as if he had caught a crayfish. I could see his whiskers. He was that close. Or was he a she? The head was not large. A female maybe, or a young dog otter. I hardly dared breathe. He dived again, slipping down into the river, leaving hardly a ripple behind him. I waited. Up he came half a minute or so later, his fur shining, his eyes bright and watching me, with something else to chew on, held in his paws, another crayfish perhaps. Our eyes met. He was still for a moment as he considered me.

Then down he went again, slipping under the water. Up he came. Down he went. Up he came. I began to count after a while. Eighty times the otter disappeared and then came back up to feed, or was it to see me? It wasn't a sighting anymore, but a meeting. The moment lasted perhaps half an hour or more. Then he was gone, and I was alone.

I passed the place again today, stopped and looked for him. I always do, but in recent times it has been mostly in the rain. Not today. Today the river sparkled with sunlight, a flurry of noisy ducks circled overhead, and I felt at last the warm breath of spring on my face.

He knows I come by most days. Maybe my Tarka will come to see me again. Hope so. How I hope so.

Where are the swallows?

I SHOULDN'T WORRY ABOUT THE SWALLOWS. THEY WILL come soon enough. There's already been word on the radio that one or two have been seen in the country, but not around here. And those few that have been seen might well have overwintered here anyway. It's happening more and more with global warming and climate change, that's what I hear. They will come when they will come. Once the bluebells are out in the woods, once the swallows have returned, then winter will truly be forgotten. A swallow would help. And one would be a start.

Eight thousand miles from southern Africa they have to fly, through rainstorms and hail and snow, over oceans and the savannah, over rainforests and deserts, to get here. What sights they must see, what stories they could tell. Would that we could understand their songs. We have a family of them who make that perilous journey every year and come home to us, Africa to Devon, every spring. Enough must have survived from their extended families for them to know the way. Bird brain indeed!

Sometimes they will build two or three nests during the months that they are with us, and they lay usually four to six eggs in each clutch, and maybe two hatchings a year, before the young are flying well enough to set off on their journey back to Africa. So we have ahead of us the joy of watching the whole story unfold in front of our eyes. We will see them arrive – soon now – and how hard they work at it, swooping down and skimming up all the mud they need, building up their nests from puddles and river-banks. There's plenty of mud about, certainly enough this year.

They'll find a safe site, high up and hidden away under a rafter at the back of our garage. Often, it's an established place they choose, one they used the year before that they restore. They'll be in and out of the garage for days on end, until their cup of clay is just as they need it to be to make a nest, neat and strong and secure. They know where to find the best mud for the nest. Once they stop their busy comings and goings, we know they'll be laying their eggs, then hatching them out. For two or three weeks we might discreetly glimpse only the head of the sitting parent bird, and then the comings and goings will start all over again, as they both busy themselves feeding the chicks. And we will witness again the gaping insatiable beaks filling the nest, letting the parents know noisily that they are hungry, again.

Then we will be able to watch the drama of first flight, of all the chicks learning to take off, fly, line up on the telephone wire, growing every day in agility and strength, in self-confidence, in their ability to look after themselves.

But where are the swallows? Will they be back? Will they find their garage home again? Many don't make it, I know that. I just hope ours do.

Ten years ago we put up the garage in the garden, not for them, but for a car. But because of the swallows, we now never use it for the car and we don't shut the doors of the garage. We leave the doors open for them.

When the swallows first came, they took us by surprise. They just arrived one spring ten years ago and claimed their place, making the garage their own. They simply set about building their nests, and that was even before the building of the garage was finished. It is very expensive accommodation for them, but it's been worth every penny to have them living with us.

The arrival of the first swallow is always eagerly awaited. Some wish-fulfilling has already happened. You can't mistake the graceful flight of a swallow. They slice through the air, they weave about the sky, the constant weaving, I suspect, a natural defence tactic to avoid the hawks. They skim, they soar, they swoop, often screeching for joy as they fly. You feel their pleasure in flying. They are supreme acrobats.

And they do love to sit on our telephone wire, singly or in numbers. So yesterday when I saw a small bird sitting where they often sit on the telephone wire near the garage, and surveying the view towards Dartmoor, I was sure it had to be the first swallow. Clare – always more sceptical, more right – said it couldn't be, not yet. She came to look. 'Long-tailed tit,' she told me. She meant the bird, I think. And so it proved. Very annoying. We shall have to wait a little longer for our swallows.

On the other hand, we have discovered our first flowering bluebell. Clare verifies it as such. This season-changing bluebell has appeared at the foot of our gatepost, just the one, the first of the spring, and in our gateway. That bluebell chose us! So, much rejoicing today. We took a picture of the moment, of the flower. We might have to wait a while for her thousands upon thousands of cousins to show themselves in Bluebell Wood.

*

The effort to endure this long tail of winter – cold wind again today, but at least no rain – goes on all around us on the farm. I just saw the children from a Plymouth school, out with Simon, walking out into the wind over Pond Field, sacks of food for the sheep over their shoulders, and the ewes were following on, hard on their heels and hopeful, the whole flock of them bleating in chorus, letting the children know they were in urgent need of sustenance. The ewes each have one or two lambs to look after, and some are already keen to feed at the troughs alongside their mothers.

I stay a while to watch, unnoticed, remembering how it was to be out there all those years, with the children, through every lambing season; how tired the farmers are at this time of year. When you keep stock through the winter months there is just so much that needs doing all the time, morning, noon and night, and so much anxiety to deal with. Both Simon and Adam have families, so late nights and early mornings with lambs and children have been constant.

When I hear the children shaking out their sacks, their laughter pealing in the wind, I think of Dylan Thomas and his poem 'Fern Hill'. He had been a farm boy once on his aunt's farm in Wales, and never forgot it. His words still sing for us the wondrous song of his childhood. It begins:

'Now as I was young and easy under the apple boughs,
    About the lilting house and happy as the grass was green . . .'

Spring

Green and golden are the colours of Dylan Thomas's poem. Green and golden are memories for me of working with the children out on the farm. And 'green and golden' speaks too of the time the Plymouth children are having. They're having the time of their lives right now as I write this, all of them out there in their skipping wellies – no, not poetic licence, some do skip in wellies, promise.

The sight of the children walking out over the fields is a timely reminder to me of all the work that is going on day in day out on this farm and on all farms, hampered this year by months of almost continuous rain. It is the season of hope and renewal, but every year coming out of the winter into spring is a struggle, hard to endure physically and mentally, fraught with anxiety and difficulty. Every day there is elation and every day there is disappointment. That's the way of farming, especially at this time of year. There is birth, there is death. But having the children on the farm with us can and does lift our spirits.

Of all their experiences on the farm, it is perhaps witnessing, even helping, with the birth of a lamb or calf that will stay with them. Typically, the ewe will be found away from the others, often lying close to the shelter of a hedge. The great thing is not to disturb her, to let her give birth without anxiety. But if labour has been going on too long, or she looks unusually uncomfortable, then that's the time to give her a hand.

Feeling inside tells us if it might be a multiple birth and triplets are not uncommon – but they can be more complicated and more tiring for the mother and farmer both. It's important to discover if the lamb is strong, is presenting well. Farmers like Simon and Adam are used to birthing ewes and cows, used to explaining to the children what is going on. It is tense sometimes, but usually all is well. And the relief is palpable when it's over and the mother is up and licking over her newborn.

Mostly we are still lambing indoors at the moment. It's just too wet and cold outside. Newborns have to be kept warm and out of rain and wind. This morning, we had another birth – the children again found me in the vegetable garden picking kale, and told me on their way home to Nethercott for breakfast. It happened overnight in the barn, a large, single ewe lamb. The mother lambed by herself. They found ewe and lamb standing there impatient to be let out to the grass. It's a dry morning, with some warmth in the sun, so Simon will let her out later for a while.

So it was a good morning to welcome more new young farmers to the farm. These days, the children's first job on the farm after breakfast is to turn all the ewes with older lambs out to grass. A dry day of sun is what the sheep really need. We don't like to keep them inside any longer than we have to. They are only in the barn to bond and to shelter the youngest and weakest lambs from the worst of the weather, and from predators. There are too many foxes about. Foxes, and badgers too, are the worst culprits. Once they have killed they will often come back for more.

We are turning them out into the little paddock beside Burrow, the cottage where Adam lives. It's sheltered there, and close at hand so he can keep an eye on them, and is surrounded by tall trees that protect them from the worst of the prevailing weather, which comes to us mostly from the south-west. The trouble is that all too quickly this paddock is becoming bare of grass now. They need to move out onto the fresh pasture of our largest field, Burrow Brimclose. But they are more exposed there to the weather and to predators. It's a balance of risks.

Herding the ewes and lambs from field to field, as we often do, is a slow and noisy affair. The lambs are constantly becoming confused and separated, endlessly losing their mothers and searching frantically for them, bleating to be recognised and reunited. The ewes are equally upset, equally noisy. Ewes and lambs recognise one another through sound initially, and then through scent. The lambs often try to suckle at once when they find their mothers, for reassurance as much as hunger, and will always be rejected and butted away by a mother that is not theirs; so it takes a while for them to get sorted out. But in the end they all find one another, and calm down, then gradually make their way in the direction of the new field, where the ewes discover fresh grass and the lambs can suckle as they graze. Peace and quiet contentment can return to the flock.

Lambing may be almost over, but there is always farm work to be done. The children have been barrowing manure onto our autumn raspberry beds. Our tractor can't get into the old walled vegetable garden, and the only way to bring manure into the garden is with wheelbarrows through the doorway, and down the narrow path under the apple trees. Besides them, all that is showing above ground at the moment are small 'stumps' of last year's canes of raspberries, and the first green shoots of this year's growth.

It is hard for the children to imagine as they tip the barrows of muck on the bed that the canes and their heavy crop of raspberries will be taller than them in a matter of a few weeks, that in a few months the vegetables will be growing everywhere.

Other children have been lifting rogue potatoes that avoided being harvested last year. Lifting them is a

Spring

popular job, a bit like digging for treasure! Worms are great treasures! Clearing the ground of them will allow us to plant out new season crops shortly.

*

Mornings have been overcast again and turning to showers and blustery rain. As usual, the children start every day feeding the pigs, poultry, cows and sheep. Our latest batch of chicks have started hatching in the incubator. The children love following the hatching process, from collecting fertile eggs from the hens 'paired up' with the cockerel, to candling the eggs – shining a light on the egg to check development – and finally inspecting any that have hatched and huddle under the warmth of the heat lamp.

Other jobs often include making up vegetable boxes from the garden, harvesting salad leaves in the shelter of the polytunnel. That polytunnel is one of the best places to be on a day of rain and wind.

Every day still brings more unwelcome rain, leaving lambs and ewes looking wet and bedraggled, their fleeces stained with mud. A pair of older lambs found under a hedge this afternoon were looking severely chilled, shivering with cold, so they and their mother had to be brought inside at once. Weak they might have been, but lambs can give the dog a good run around, and these two did. Lambs can be extraordinarily difficult to move until they get used to the dog.

We've been planting lots of trees with the children over the winter. They were planted out in small fenced-off areas, just 30 to 40 centimetres high, known as 'bare-root whips', to provide cover eventually for cows and sheep. The fencing will come down once the trees are mature enough in ten or fifteen years, by which time there will be wild areas all around them; this will benefit insect life, of course, which benefits us all. In fact, when we planted them, the children struggled to believe these were trees at all, whether they were alive even. They looked more like dead twigs blown down from the trees during a storm. What the children do learn as they plant them is just how important trees are to sustaining our planet, and how every tree planted will help, how *they* have helped.

But we have already started seeing more life in some of these little sticks. Small, bright, glossy leaflets are appearing. Mainly hawthorn and elder are awakening from winter, but it won't be long before the other species follow. In the hedgerows surrounding the fields, the children are starting to see flowers, not just the bright yellow of the gorse, but blackthorn too. Blackthorn, always early to blossom, will be an early source of nectar for bees as they become more active in the days to come.

Our beehives haven't been opened up and inspected yet. It is still too early to expose them and their brood to this inclement weather. We're still having to feed the bees as there is as yet relatively little wild forage out there for them. However, an ear close to the brood box can detect bee activity within all three hives, which is good news. Once we have a fine day, we will be able to watch them flying in and out. It'll be so good to see them out and about and being busy again.

Critical to the children's week on the farm is the variety of tasks they have to undertake. It is a truly mixed farm. Feeding the pigs is hugely popular, especially the piglets. They had to say goodbye to some today. No tears, but a clearer understanding of how farms bring us food, animal or vegetable. Five of our oldest litter of piglets were sold away to new homes. We shall miss them, but they are a good strong litter and will be grown on and looked after well by local smallholders who are rearing pork for their families, friends and neighbours.

I still listen every day for the tweet of the first swallow, and I'm always on the lookout for one sitting up there on the telephone wire near their garage. I know too that one swallow doesn't make a summer, but a sight or sound of one would make my spring.

You have to smile

WE'VE BEEN WAKING TO DRY AND SUNNY MORNINGS for a couple of days in succession now. The lambs are leaping about in frisky gangs these days, playing chase, learning how to head-butt. They're no longer lying there, hunched and sheltering from the wind and rain. The children try to count the lambs on their afternoon check of the livestock. They check especially round the hedges. Counting the lambs when they are haring around in crazy circles is a tricky job, but the children love it.

It's been officially spring since 20 March, weeks ago now. In the wind there are still some chilly days, but we're beginning already not to bother with coats and hats when we go out, which is unwise, I'm told. Clare has a granny saying about that too: 'Ne'er cast a clout till May be out.' And of course there's truth in that. The sunshine and blue sky may look like summer, but it won't become summer until 20 June, and that's a long way off. Between now and then, the brighter weather can be treacherous. So I'll do as the saying says, and keep my coat on for a while yet.

The truth is that, in this country, we have to be sceptical about the weather. The months and the seasons are just not to be trusted. I grew up with a ditty about that, 'A Song of the Weather', by Flanders and Swann it was. I've never forgotten it.

> January brings the snow,
> Makes your feet and fingers glow.
> February's ice and snow,
> Freeze the toes right off your feet
>
> Welcome March with wintry wind,
> Would thou wert not so unkind.
> April brings the sweet spring showers,
> On and on, for hours and hours.
>
> Farmers fear unkindly May,
> Frost by night, and hail by day.
> June just rains and never stops,
> Thirty days and spoils the crops.

May proper: You have to smile

In July the sun is hot.
Is it shining? No, it's not.
August's cold and dank and wet,
Brings more rain than any yet.

Bleak September's mist and mud,
Is enough to chill the blood.
Then October adds a gale,
Wind and slush and rain and hail.

Dark November brings the fog,
Should not do it to a dog.
Freezing wet December, then
Bloody January again.

January brings the snow,
Makes your feet and fingers glow . . .

We've had to smile our way through long days of wind
and rain, of grey skies and mud. But now we can begin at
long last to cast away the gloom of winter, when it was
such an effort to keep smiling sometimes. Our spirits rise
daily with every bank of daffodils we see, with the sight
of the darting wren building her nest by the front door,
with the pied wagtails washing themselves diligently in
the gutters, with the blossom of the plum tree blooming

in our garden, with the garden pots full of Delft-blue hyacinths, anemones purple and white, crocus gold and lavender blue, with the tulips almost there, with the rhubarb and the spinach beginning to grow again, and the blackcurrant and gooseberry bushes bursting with new life, with fruit soon enough.

It's true that grey and cold seem to dull the world about us, and we can be inclined to lower our mood, to stop us taking notice. I find this particularly in cities, where I'm just trying to get from A to B, and to avoid cars and cyclists and joggers. But with the sun out, I stop and stare more. I've been up in London again, to see my family, and have been walking along the Thames to the Underground.

I must have stood there by the river for half an hour or more watching the swans cruising by, the crows and gulls mobbing one another, the rowers gliding past, the heron standing waiting in the shallows for some poor unsuspecting fish to pass by, the ducks pairing up and squabbling, and the willows and poplars already green with spring, the parakeets flying above me, bright green, fast and straight and loud. I'm suddenly noticing all of it. Now the dull light of winter is almost gone, I'm more aware. It's as if I'm waking up, like the world about me.

I walked this way often in the winter months, and I

hardly gave any of it a look then. But now, everything about me has new colour and new life. People are laughing, some as raucous and as joyful as the parakeets, like the children in the fields back home in Devon. I'm hoping that there'll be bluebells in the wood when I get back, and with any luck the swallows won't be long now. I've been tracking them in my head. I think they must be over Spain by now. I've been looking to see early swallows in London, and I'm quite glad I haven't seen any. I want the first one I see to be our swallow at home, flying into our garage. If the first swallow comes when I'm not there, I shall not be best pleased.

*

We were back home in Devon before the first swallow finally arrived. But Clare, digging more compost into her flower bed, saw it first, and called me downstairs. I thought it was for a cup of coffee. I was deep into writing this, so at first was slow to respond. Then she called up and said she had a surprise. That sounded more interesting than just a cup of coffee. So down I went. She took me out into the garden and told me to stand by the garage and wait, and be patient.

And in moments, there the swallow was, swooping

down over us and up over the garage. Then there were two of them. After a brief flying display, they settled alongside one another, folded their wings and surveyed their Devon home, reclaiming it. Clare and I had no words. I could think of only one thing to do. I clapped quietly, almost silently, to welcome them, to celebrate their 8,000-mile journey, and their arrival, bringing the spring with them. We had tea outside afterwards, on the bench, and sat there watching them coming and going. We clinked teacups and felt all was right with the world.

And a week or so later, out on my walk through the woods, the massed bluebells were there waiting for me, covering the ground entirely from the stream at the bottom of the woods up to where I was standing under the beech trees at the top. I breathed in the scent of the bluebells, breathed in deep of them. It is always a marvel, that first time I see them en masse like this. I walked on, careful not to tread on any of them, past the badger sett, and keeping close to the hedge bright with yellow gorse, tripping more than once over fallen twigs, so intent was I on feasting my eyes on the bluebells, until I reached the gate. And there beyond it was the shining river, the Torridge running as sweet and soft as the Thames, but with no joggers or cyclists to bother me. A jay flew off, cackling. A blackbird sang her song of gladness. They always sing of gladness. Heaven it was to hear that, sheer heaven.

And then I discovered that the tadpoles must have hatched out in what was left of that puddle down by the gateway, and just in time too. It has been drying out fast. I did think, as I walked back home along the river, that it was possible the heron had visited them in the puddle, but I preferred not to think of that, and certainly not on the day the bluebells had come into their own.

Closer to the river, I was treated to a spectacular display. Swallows and martins and swifts were flying together over the river. It seemed as if the whole world was celebrating. I remembered seeing the children skipping for joy in their wellies. It seemed like a good idea, and no one was watching. I did a few skips. Not so easy as it used to be, but the child in me loved doing it.

As I came skipping merrily, but more cautiously these days, down the hill towards the puddle by the gateway where I had found the frogspawn a while ago, a duck flew up in alarm out of the nearby hedge, quacking frantically. I thought this was a strange place for a duck to be, or to nest. It was at least three hundred metres from the river. So I looked closer into the hedge. There, hidden deep in the centre of it, was a nest. I counted nine white eggs. The duck was circling high over the river. I walked away at once, keeping an eye on her as she flew, sure she was watching me, hoping to goodness I hadn't lingered by the nest too long, that my curiosity would not cause her to desert her eggs.

Five minutes later she was still up there, circling. I was far away by now, and willing her all the time to go back to her eggs. That was when I noticed a heron, flying high up over the river and away, far away by now from the hideaway duck's nest in the hedgerow. I heaved a sigh of relief. The eggs were safe. I turned away and kept walking along the river, looking out, as I often do, for a kingfisher, or even an otter maybe. I almost forgot about the duck, about the heron.

But then I did look back, just once, and I wished I hadn't. The heron was flying low and slow along the hedgerow, hunting like a drone, searching. There was no sign of the mother duck. If she was back on her eggs again, all would be well, if only she stayed sitting stock-still. It was her only hope of saving her eggs, her duck-lings-to-be. I could not watch anymore. I knew what my moment of absurd frivolity might have caused, panicking her away noisily from her nest as I had, knew the heron must have been watching me peering into the nest, waiting for me to be gone. I hurried home, trying not to think about it.

On the way back up the track I passed a cluster of early purple orchids, 'goosey ganders' as they are sometimes

known – 'long purples' as Shakespeare called them in *Hamlet*. My thoughts turned to Shakespeare then, and the familiar lines from his well-known sonnet, number 18. It wasn't summer, but it felt like it.

> Shall I compare thee to a summer's day?
> Thou art more lovely and more temperate:
> Rough winds do shake the darling buds of May,
> And summer's lease hath all too short a date.

He has a way of reminding us how the seasons move on, how they mark the rhythm of our lives, each season, like each life, quickly over, how we should make the most of all of them. But springtime, like youth and childhood, is the prologue to life, and must be lived to the full, whatever the weather, whatever the state of the world. It is a time for looking forward, in hope. It always has been.

MAY STILL

Living memory

As a child, I don't think I had any early under-standing of the seasons. I lived them, of course, knew well that the cold gave my toes chilblains, knew there were sometimes leaves to scuffle through, that I could play out late when the days were warm and long, knew there was a time when flowers and trees blossomed, when birds nested. But I was hardly aware of the rhythm of the seasons.

I suppose it's not surprising. We have to have lived a few years to comprehend how and why the seasons happen. But as children we live intensely for the now, and have little sense of the passing of time. I lived my most formative years in a place almost as remote as where I live now. My childhood home in Bradwell on the east coast was most certainly just as 'far from the madding crowd' as my home now in deepest Devon. I know now that I lived my first springs there.

Spring

It was out on my favourite walk in and around my home in Bradwell that I first discovered countryside, down the track through the hedgeless, treeless fields, past the ancient Saxon chapel of St Peter's to the sea wall and the great brown soupy North Sea beyond. It was the walk that was to change my life.

That was where I saw my first hares, which I had thought must be rabbits. I had stopped often to watch rabbits, running around out on the stubble. I'd seen rabbits in the garden at home before, and foxes, and a badger once. I'd seen hedgehogs too. That sighting of hares was the first time I had to stop and stare.

I only knew they were hares because a farmer on his tractor, coming down the track, told me so. 'Mad March hares! See 'em, son!' he said. 'And they don't know it's not March neither. Halfway through April it is. Mad as hatters, all of them. Look at 'em!'

And sure enough they were jigging about in crazy circles, chasing one another, jumping up and down, and two of them were up on their hind legs and looked as if they were boxing one another. I'd never heard of a hare, never seen such a thing before. The farmer soon went off with a laugh and a wave on his tractor, and left me alone with the hares. I could hear the sea in the distance, and the screech of swallows swooping around St Peter's Chapel.

I stayed there, watching all this miraculous display, quite unable to walk away. I was transfixed. And then, as I stood there, I heard a cuckoo calling to me from the reed beds by the sea wall. I listened, echoing his call back to him, until he called no more. I remember running all the way home to tell everyone about my cuckoo, and the hares and the swallows over St Peter's. I was met by scepticism. Too early for a cuckoo, my aunties said. And hares don't really get up and box on their hind legs, it was just a legend, and no one else had seen a swallow arriving yet. I'd seen and heard all of it, and no one believed me. It was more of Michael's made-up tales. And it's true, even then I was doing that. But that was not a tale. It was a memory, and one I've never forgotten.

Those hares, those swallows, that cuckoo, that walk down the track out to the chapel that morning, along with Clare's walks on the wild side in Devon, brought us ultimately to teaching and to spend our lives introducing children to an awareness of the wildness of nature and the joys of discovering the world about us. We owe her walks of discovery as a child, that cuckoo, and those hares and swallows, a great deal.

But memory is indiscriminate and has its uncomfortable side. We don't forget our shames. Ignorance is no excuse, but I was unaware of the seasons when I used to climb trees to go looking for birds' eggs. Egg collecting was as popular as collecting stamps. I knew how to blow them, lay them neatly on cotton wool in the special box I kept under my bed. I'd swap eggs with my friends. My favourite, I remember, was a wren's egg, light brown it was, and as I found it, in its tiny woven nest. There can be no more perfect springtime creation. I shudder when I think of it, of my treasured pride and joy, and the harm I did.

The nesting wrens above our front door are back again, and trusting us not to meddle, not to intrude, to respect their privacy. I can't forget the duck that I frightened off her nest, off her eggs. I'm a lot more careful now with our wrens. I think both the parent birds are darting in and out, but I'm not really sure if it's just one or both of them. The female might be sitting already. In which case it's less than two weeks till the eggs hatch out.

And every day I'm seeing more wild flowers. In Candlelight Meadow, across the lane from our cottage, and down in the Okement valley, there are cuckooflowers growing in among the rushes, and growing in greater numbers than we've ever seen before. They are mauve in colour and easily distinguishable. The wild flowers on the wetter fields on the farm are definitely more plentiful. I think they must have had more chance to flower because the fields have been left longer empty of cows. It's been far too wet, of course, to let the cows out to graze the more low-lying fields. We used to have curlews in Candlelight Meadow years ago, in among the cuckoo-flowers, but not for a while. Curlews like marshy fields. Perhaps they'll be back one day.

We miss the curlews, and we miss the larks too, that used to nest on the higher fields on the farm. I remember watching them rise up so high towards the sun until I was left only with their song. But I haven't seen or heard a lark for years now. No doubt their disappearance from the countryside is in part due to climate change, but it's also due to the change in modern farming methods too. When both curlews and larks are back again, we shall know we are doing things right again.

But we have more swallows. Word is out. Swallows have been seen in numbers flying over the Torridge river, our neighbours tell us. It'll be so good to have them back with us. In a way, I'm surprised they've come back at all. We have a cold wind still blowing in, another named gale, Kathleen this time. There have been so many gales coming in one after the other. The river is bank-high again and rushing along.

It doesn't feel like it in the wind, but it seems that the air must be warming. Blossoms are everywhere, pear and apple blossoming in abundance, but sadly blown off and scattered all too soon. The wind comes in ferocious gusts, shaking trees and house alike. The big ash tree has been roaring all night long. We felt storm-tossed last night, or, as Ted Hughes puts it, 'the house has been far out at sea'.

I thought I caught a glimpse of a young stag in the woods today, with antlers to be proud of, but he was gone quickly before I saw him again. No fish are jumping in the river yet, but there have been salmon sighted further downriver, which is good. They have been releasing salmon parr in large numbers into the Torridge, doing all they can to restock the river. People are working hard to put things right. We need the water to be clean, with no run-off of manure or fertiliser from the fields, with no releases from the sewers. The land will heal, the creatures will thrive, but only if we make it happen. There has been much damage done, from fouling our rivers to stealing eggs. And we've all been doing it. We have much to repair. Nature renews and repairs herself every spring, helps herself, but we must not hinder her anymore. We have to renew our bond with the natural world, with the rhythm of the seasons.

*

I went up to read this evening to the children from the Plymouth school who've been with us on the farm. I like to do that – it reminds me of how I began my storytelling life when I was a teacher in a primary school fifty years ago. Hope they enjoyed it as much as I did. By all accounts, they had a happy week despite the changeable weather. They all saw a lamb born, something they'll never forget. I saw their coach going home down the lane the next day. Lots of tearful waving. It reminded me of a poem by my favourite mentor and writer, Robert Louis Stevenson.

Farewell to the Farm

The coach is at the door at last;
The eager children, mounting fast
And kissing hands, in chorus sing:
Goodbye, goodbye, to everything!

To house and garden, field and lawn,
The meadow-gates we swang upon,
To pump and stable, tree and swing,
Goodbye, goodbye, to everything!

And fare you well for evermore
O ladder at the hayloft door,
O hayloft where the cobwebs cling,
Goodbye, goodbye, to everything!

Spring

Crack goes the whip, and off we go;
The trees and houses smaller grow;
Last, round the woody turn we sing:
Goodbye, goodbye, to everything!

STILL MAY

'Most acceptable'

In Bluebell Wood, the bluebells are back. It's not a carpet of bluebells, it's a fanfare of bluebells, announcing themselves to the world with a flourish of sudden colour. I'd forgotten how deep a blue they are en masse, how sweet and surprising the scent of them. How different this wood is to me now as I walk through, how different it must be, too, to the cackling jays, the twitching squirrels, the disappearing deer, the slumbering badgers, the foxes out hunting after rabbits and voles and moles. The trees, all clothed now in new leaf, are whispering to one another in open admiration, echoing my own. It's a haven of wondrous new beauty for all of us.

Just now I stood and watched two swallows sitting side by side on the telephone wire, surveying our garage, their summer home. How does it work with swallows? Did these two leave here last autumn, winter together in

Africa, debate together when was the right moment to leave on their perilous journey back to Devon, to our garage? Or is only one of them the surviving swallow of last year's pair, who has found another good companion, another mate, who is therefore bringing along a stranger to last year's nesting site. Is one proposing to the other up there on the telephone wire to make a new home in our garage? Does the stranger have another place in mind? Will they argue, will they decide to stay?

They're sitting quite close to one another. Their body language tells me they're not arguing about it, just discussing. The old nests, last year's nests, are still there waiting, needing much renovation. Plenty of muddy puddles about for that. Another wren – I don't think it's our house wren – has recently taken over one of their old nests, and has adapted it neatly, fitting it out with mostly moss and soft dry grasses. We had three or four pairs of swallows nesting last year. Mustn't be greedy. One pair, this pair, will be fine, or – as we say in Devon – 'most acceptable'.

They take off and fly away together out over the sheep field, around the cottage chimney and the garage, and swoop down to have a closer look inside the garage. I think they're checking it out. Then soon enough, they're back on the telephone wire discussing it. I leave them to it. I know I mustn't intrude. Just being there watching can do that. I have the feeling they know what

I'm thinking, what I'm hoping. They certainly know I'm watching. I leave them to it.

The yearly marvel of the arrival of our swallows has got me thinking, about migration, how migration is about need, the need to survive, to find safety, to escape, to feed and to breed. The swifts will be here soon. They like to spend the summer down the lane on Simon's farm at Bridgetown. They've always nested there, in the barns. You can see them too swooping around the church tower in Iddesleigh, soaring high over the village green. No one has seen one yet, but they'll be here soon enough now. The house martins are about already, the yellow wagtails, the black caps and tree pipits – all of them migrating birds, all coming to us because they must. In order to survive they must breed. They need a temporary home. Here, the next generation will be hatched out, will learn to fly, to grow up. How welcome they are. How they enrich our lives.

A few years ago, in a neighbouring village whose name I will not mention, I saw a woman, broom in hand, reaching up and systematically knocking down house martins' nests under the eaves of her house. I'd noticed them often, as I drove by, flying back and forth, busy building their meticulous nests of cupped mud. I was enraged by this thoughtless act of destruction. But I buttoned my lip, and drove on by, looking the other way. To my shame I said nothing, did nothing.

Spring

Cuckoos, of course, are not considerate migrants. They have, as we know, one deeply unpleasant habit, so unpleasant I thought it deserved a poem.

Cuckoo, in the depths of the wood

It's a long-haul flight, I'm telling you . . . Cuckoo!
But a cuckoo has to cuckoo, if you see what I'm
    saying . . . Cuckoo!
Even if we have to travel far . . . Cuckoo!
And it's worth it when we get there . . . Cuckoo!

The people love my song, listen for it, echo it
    back . . . Cuckoo!
Must be spring, they say. How they love my song . . .
    Cuckoo!
Cuckoo, I call, from the dark of the woods, over the
    bright fields . . . Cuckoo!
Down the swirling river, over the whispering
    reeds . . . Cuckoo!

I'll lay my egg in some lucky warbler's nest . . .
    Cuckoo!
Small nest, big egg! Lovely little bird a warbler . . .
    Cuckoo!
But not the brightest . . . Cuckoo!

They'll feed my little cuckoo all he can swallow . . .
   Cuckoo!

Work themselves to death . . . Cuckoo!
Grow my chick into a giant . . . Cuckoo!
No little warbler siblings allowed . . . Cuckoo!
Job done! Home again! . . . Cuckoo!

Cuckoo! . . . Cuckoo! . . . Cuckoo! . . . Cuckoo!

Of course, migration goes on in our rivers and streams too, but largely unseen. Young eels – elvers – are born thousands of miles away in the Sargasso Sea in the Atlantic Ocean, and swim all that way to us to feed and grow in our rivers, in the Torridge and Okement. Sadly, like so much of our wildlife, they too are endangered. Eels are prime prey for the herons and otters and cormorants in the rivers. They would not be there at all without the eels. Lose the eels and we lose them.

I have migration on my mind too, because I saw my first salmon yesterday, down on the Torridge, on Monument Marsh. I caught only a glimpse, but a glimpse was enough. I was alerted by the widening ripple of a fish feeding, probably a brown trout, I thought, or a rainbow trout. There are mayflies hatching out now over the river – I'd noticed them before. But this was my first sighting, that day on my walk of a ripple, a sure sign that a fish was there and feeding. Look long enough, patiently enough, at a ripple like that and you might see a fish rising again to feed. I didn't have to be that patient. A few moments later, a salmon rose up briefly and showed himself, showed me the shining curve of his back, and the tell-tale tail. A young salmon, a veritable salmon!

It's a rare enough sight these days too, and a reminder to me of the cycle of life of this remarkable fish. Hidden from us, but happening close to us, this fish hatched out here in our river, by parents who returned from the Atlantic Ocean to their own place of birth, laid eggs, fertilised the eggs, one of which became the young fish I just saw. He will stay in the river and feed for maybe three years, then swim back to the estuary, grow there into a fully adult fish and swim out into the wide Atlantic Ocean, only to return a while later to play out the same drama of cyclical migration.

Swallow, swift, cuckoo, eel, salmon, us. All of us migrants, each in our own way. These regular walks down by the river so often take my mind in a wander, remind me of the lives all about us in the wild, taken so easily for granted, remind me too of those people before me who have been here, family, friends, the farmers, the anglers, the writers, the children who come to us from the cities. They are all companions on my walks. I am never alone.

Henry Williamson was here in my neck of the woods, treading the same path. His best-loved book, *Tarka the Otter*, gave its name to the Tarka Trail, a footpath that takes the walker through the farm, down along the rivers where Tarka lived, in the story. Williamson knew the Torridge river and its life and otters intimately.

Tarka the Otter may be the book most closely associated with the river, but it's another of Williamson's books that is not often read, but for me is even more remarkable, *Salar the Salmon*. It takes place entirely underwater. It feels as if it was actually written underwater. It is a feat of quite extraordinary observation and imagination, following the life of a salmon from the river to the sea.

But of course it's those who live and work by the rivers that know them more intimately than any writer could, in all seasons, in flood and in drought, in all weathers, in all moods. On the farm, it is Simon and Adam who know them best. The cows and calves, sheep and lambs are all out now, at last, grazing the spring grass, and have to be checked and counted regularly, often with the children, as part of their farm work. When the river is in spate, they have to be out there to move them to safety on higher ground.

The next city school has just arrived for their week on the farm, from London this time. The children troop down the hill with Simon as usual to check on the cows and calves on Monument Marsh, the field at the confluence of the Torridge and Okement rivers. Regular checking on the newborn calves – and there are now dozens of them – is very important. Each birth is a relief and a joy, to the farmer, to anyone who witnesses it, to the mother cow.

Outcomes are not always happy. To lose a calf at birth is always a deep sadness for everyone there. We lost one only a few days ago. A strange day it was that began with the rare and exciting sighting of a huge bird flying high over the river, too high for a heron. First thoughts were that it must be a stork. We saw a stork only once before, but they are seen around here in Devon more than they were. This bird looked similar, a huge wingspan, a supreme flyer, but it did not look white enough to be a stork. It was grey, more like a heron, but too big for a heron. It took a while to believe it, but it was a crane, a common crane, which is far from common. I'd never seen one before in my life. A neighbour who knows his birds really well confirmed he'd seen it too, and that it was a crane. Cranes, he told me, are making a comeback in this country after near extinction.

An hour or two after the exhilaration of seeing the crane came the tragedy of the calf being born dead. With every birth on the farm there is expectation of life, of hope fulfilled. This birth looked simple enough, taking no longer than normal, an experienced mother, the farmer there to help. Once born, the calf lay there, still. Efforts were made to clear her nostrils so she could breathe. But she didn't breathe. Everything was done to stir her into life. But there was no life, only stillness. It left us all empty, tearful. We know it happens, but that does not help when it does.

In writing this, I am trying to think of the crane soaring up there majestically, effortlessly, but the memory of the calf lying there, still, silent, lifeless, comes back to me. This is the hard side of farming. The ups and downs can be difficult to endure. We have the compensations of living in a beautiful place, in peace and quiet. But for many it is a seven day a week job, and maybe fourteen hours a day. The children learn, when they come to stay, that wind or shine, for the farmer the animals, the crops, have to come first. So, with the sheep and cows outside as they are now, there is a twice daily strict count of the calves and their mothers to be done. The animals can go down to drink in the river, but can sometimes get across to the other side and become separated. A calf would then be in great danger, and might try in desperation to get back across the river where it is too deep.

And here on Monument Marsh there is a granite cross that was put up, over a hundred years ago now, to remember a young man, called George Christopher

Easton, who drowned in the river while fishing. It's both
a memorial and a warning. Simon's late father, David
Ward, thought it might be a good idea to have an annual
gathering of families down by the cross, so he is remembered. We play games, have a picnic down by the river.
In future, when we have our gathering down by the
cross, we will be remembering both David and George
Christopher Easton, each in a very different way – one
we knew well, the other not at all.

*

There's a temptation to think of this time of year as a
kind of interval between winter and summer. It's not. It's
like saying that youth is simply a prelude of age. Yes,
young people might be impatient to grow up and become
adults. And yes, each year we are impatient for summer
to be here. But to be strong and fulfilled in life, young
people must have time and space for growth, to be encouraged to grow into knowledge and understanding and
awareness of the world about them and of themselves
and of the part they can play in it. That growing period
is not to be rushed through. It is, like spring, the most
formative part of new life, not a mere prologue.

Spring

Sun and the summer warmth are here again. The cold winds have blown away. Dartmoor is there under blue skies every day. And the blackbird sings to me every morning. The beeches and chestnut trees and even the oaks are coming into glorious leaf. We've seen our first meadow brown butterflies. The swallows are in and out of the garage all day and every day. And today in the lane down to the river, I saw a grass snake basking in the sun, unfearful of me, unwilling to move. I stepped over him.

Butterflies, swallows, buzzards, snakes, they all know that summer is here. We have to believe it, I too. The world is ready now for the next movement of the symphony of the seasons.

The year's turned round again. I know the world is troubled and sad, but when I look about me, and breathe in all the wonders, I know too that all shall be well.

Sumer is icumen in

SUMER IS ICUMEN IN

Summer is a coming in,
Loudly sing, Cuckoo!
Seed grows and meadow blooms
As the world springs anew
Sing, cuckoo!
The ewe bleats after the lamb,
The cow lows after the calf,
The bullock stirs, the stag farts,
Merrily sing, cuckoo!
Cuckoo, cuckoo, well you sing, cuckoo,
Don't you ever you stop now.

From a thirteenth-century song, the Summer Cannon, which
in the original begins with the words 'Sumer is icumen in',
a song to celebrate spring and the arrival of summer soon.

The goldfinches that came in their dozens every morning during the cold weather to our bird feeder for their sunflower hearts are now back. They're out in numbers on our lawn, feasting on the dandelion seeds. And I see they're busy nesting in the hedge, too, just below my writing room window.

Out in the field beyond the hedge, another cow calved yesterday, and all is well. The calf is up and about, investigating a new world. The mother is grazing nonchalantly. She's done it all before. Calving has had its ups and downs. All the other births have gone well, mothers and calves up and about and happy. Fifteen more cows still to calve.

We were having a cup of tea outside. I had to wear my hat, the sun was that strong. We were sitting there, looking out towards Dartmoor, and thinking aloud how lucky we were to be alive, to be living here. Between us and Dartmoor there is a wide valley of fields and trees, with the Okement river running through, hidden now that most of the trees are in full leaf.

Some might think of the landscape as rather understated. Painters, and some tourists, might prefer the dramatic mountains of Wales, or the splendid hills and glens of the Scottish Borders, or the lakes of the Highlands, or the glorious coastline of Cornwall. Ours is a comparatively unknown corner of England. There are few visitors, few holiday homes, and we are miles and miles from a main road. It's an inconvenient place. But that's the joy of it, the peace and quiet.

Drinking our tea, with a 180-degree view of Dartmoor fifteen miles away, we can count only two small houses in the distance. The countryside is much as it must have been a thousand and more years ago. It's a man-made landscape, the forests cut down and the hedges built by our Bronze Age forebears. They judiciously chose to settle here where it was remote and therefore safe, where water was plentiful, where the rivers ran through, for themselves and their animals. Later generations built the church and village of Iddesleigh, making tracks and roads, and planting trees. The city children were the last to do this, not that long ago. Like the farmers before them, they've left their mark, each tree a contribution to the future of the whole.

I was sitting there contemplating, as many of us do, how the clouds above us create an ever-changing meta-morphosis: a roaring polar bear becomes a map of Australia becomes a spreading chestnut tree, becomes the face of my late Auntie Bessie. It was for a moment as if she had become a diva, and was singing down to me from on high. It turned out not to be my Auntie Bessie, but a buzzard, in fact two buzzards, circling up there, wings spread wide, floating on the thermals, exulting in it, in feeling the new warmth on their backs and wings. Their wings hardly moved as they soared effortlessly, ever higher, calling to one another. These are the first buzzards we've seen behaving quite like this since last summer. It's reassuring confirmation that the seasons really are changing.

They seem to be echoing just how we feel – how good it is to be alive on such a day, in such a place. Buzzards, unlike larks, do well here, seem at home here. We see them in winter months sitting like sentinels on telegraph posts. But they must survive well enough, because, come the warmer days, they are always there, claiming the skies again. They are magnificent in flight, and when they mew or cry out to one another, their echoes ring out over the hills and far away.

The crows and rooks hate them and gang up on them mercilessly. The buzzards will put up with it for a while when the crows come to harry them. The two we saw today were bullied out of their airspace and flew off in the end, but were back half an hour later, once the crows had gone, crying out to us and to the world that they had won, that patience is a virtue, and will always win in the end. Crows and rooks weren't to be seen. Buzzards had indeed won the day!

And the buzzards were up there, wheeling around, when we had our much anticipated May Day get-together up in the village, to celebrate the end of winter and the coming of summer. The buzzards were celebrating too, the swifts with them – the swifts are nesting again in the church tower. It's grand for all of us if this celebration can happen on a sunny day in spring, with the buzzards and swifts up there sharing the sky, as this year they were.

There is another purpose, too, in this village gathering. It's a chance for the community to celebrate our communal history. Way back in 1838, the villagers founded a Friendly Society. Many villages in the country did the same, but now there are just two working Friendly Societies left. They were, in effect, unions, among the very first agricultural unions. Farm workers, who were often very poorly paid and badly housed, for whom hours were long, time off rare, employment insecure, decided they needed some kind of protection against often appalling conditions of work.

So each year the Iddesleigh Friendly Society – and I'm a proud member – gathers in the village outside the pub, The Duke of York, of which, by the way, the late Ted Hughes once wrote:

When Peggy piled the dish,
And Sean pulled the cork,
The best pub in Devon
Was the Duke of York.

We have a roll call of members, about seventy in all, and most of us always there too. Some of us live in the parish, some come from far away, but have lived here or known it well. Many more of our former members are now up in the graveyard between the pub and the church. So, we're all together as we can be again, in a way. The Hatherleigh Silver Band is there, resplendent as it is possible to be in their often ill-fitting purple uniforms, and playing wonderfully well, much better than their uniforms might suggest. They lead the march of members past the crowd of villagers – crowd hardly the right word, there being fewer than a hundred people in the parish – along the road to the church, each of us wearing a club tie and a blue ribbon. There's a fine if you forget to be properly dressed, and I forgot.

Church was brief, with rousing hymns, and with a good-humoured vicar who knows it's not the occasion to take too long over his sermon. Then it's back to the pub and to lunch in the village hall. The buzzards were still up there – floating over the village, over the flag flying on the village green, over the red telephone box that now houses the village defibrillator.

It is an understated ceremony that suits the place, in its modesty, in its respect for the past and for those who worked the land and marched before us, those who tilled the soil, planted the trees, dug the ditches, trimmed the hedges, ploughed and sowed. And the

Iddesleigh Friendly Society is still doing its work of supporting farm worker members when they fall on hard times, or when helping to pay funeral expenses. The last payment I saw in the accounts we were all given at the roll call showed that when Les Curtis, good friend to so many, died – and he was the very last farm worker in the village, the last of thousands over the centuries – his funeral expenses were supported out of the Friendly Society's funds.

I'm reminded by the celebrations up in the heart of the village, near the churchyard, that time really is 'like an ever-rolling stream' and it does bear us all away, but I'm also reminded that time, like spring each year, brings new life, new strength, new hope – and summer.

Yes, indeed, 'sumer is icumen in'.

The spelling may have been different in the thirteenth century, but they felt as we feel every year, the same hope of plenty, and expectation of long bright days ahead. Vivaldi felt this too. How else could he have written his *Four Seasons*? Whatever season he had in mind when he was composing, he lived each to the full; and in doing so, he looked backwards to the seasons he had known in his life, and forward, to the next, as we all must do.

Here, echoing Antonio Vivaldi's own poem he wrote for his *Four Seasons*, is my take on the spirit of summer, the season he was looking forward to in June of 1723. And it's

Spring

summer I am looking forward to now, just as he was more than three hundred years ago.

Summer

Welcome, happy days of sun and summer.
Welcome back, you skimming swallows,
You screeching swifts,
You buntings and godwits.
How we have longed to see you again.
You found your way back to us,
You bring our summer with you,
Make our home your summer home,
Be again, our family and friends, lift our spirits,

Warm our hearts.

Here we are to greet you again.
Woken now from winter sleep.
Honeysuckle and campion,
Dog rose and foxglove,
Buttercup and daisy.
Bright-eyed daisy by day, closed tight at night,
And every morning, every dawning,
Each one gladly opened up again, by summer sun, by you.

June: Sumer is icumen in

As we are too.

Cuckoo calls, unseen, from far-off wood,
Summer's echoing herald.
Lark rises high in the blue, and is lost.
But her song still sings.
Hay dances in the warmth of the breeze,
Sways and waves with the whispering trees.
The world has come alive again,
And it is wondrous to us,
On days like this, Sweet summer,

You make it so.

We may swelter often in the heat of the day,
As we shear our sheep and make our hay.
Summer storms may flash and rumble,
Blow in wild and gusty wings,
With squally hail and lashing rain.
They can roar and rage all they like.
We do not care, it cleans the air.
We are watered afresh, filled with newness,
Like the fields, like the flowers, like the trees.

Like the whole wide world.

Spring

And to end, words from a folk song I sing sometimes, when walking and even on stage occasionally, a song by John Tams from the play of *War Horse*.

Snow Falls

And there will come a time of great plenty,
A time of good harvest and sun,
Till then put your trust in tomorrow, my friend,
For yesterday's over and done.

The snow falls, the wind calls,
And the year turns round again,
And like barleycorn who rose from the grave
A new year will rise up again.

Acknowledgements

So many have opened my eyes and mind and heart to the little corner of England I belong to, that I call home. Family, friends, farmers, writers, artists, children – they have all contributed to my life in this place, and so to this book.

Special thanks to Clare who brought us here as a family in the first place some 50 years ago, and to all the children and grandchildren and great grandchildren with whom we have shared it.

Thanks too to farmers, Adam Bratt, and to Simon Ward, and staff at Farms for City Children over the years, who have worked with all the children who have stayed and worked on the farm this last spring whilst I was writing this. Their input was inspiring, their help invaluable to me.

This is the story of one spring in my life, told in words and illustration. All the beautiful linocuts in the book were done by Charlotte Watmore, neighbour, friend and Adam's wife, who knows and loves the countryside around us as well as we do. So my special thanks to her.

I owe, and the book owes, so much to Kirty Topiwala and the great team at Hodder. We all made *Spring* together.

About the illustrator

Charlotte Whatmore is an artist who lives on the farm at Nethercott House, Devon. Nethercott overlooks Dartmoor National Park and was the first site for Farms for City Children. Charlotte's husband Adam is the farm manager at Nethercott, so Charlotte and her family are very familiar with the land that Michael describes in this story of *Spring*.

As Michael's neighbour, Charlotte is out in this same environment every day, come rain or shine. Primarily working with linocuts, she is inspired by the natural world and countryside. She strongly believes that the experiences the visiting school children get on the farm are life-changing and she feels privileged to be raising her two young children on the farm as well, with so much engagement with nature. Charlotte is regularly involved in the care of the livestock at Nethercott and keeps her own flock of rare breed Greyface Dartmoor sheep. Her sheep, along with Nethercott's flock of Whiteface Dartmoor sheep, are featured in *Spring* in Michael's anecdotes about lambing.